AT THE END OF THE DAY

AT THE END OF THE DAY

TRAVASA BUFORD

TNHB Inspirations, LLC
Huntsville, Alabama

AT THE END OF THE DAY

Published by
TNHB Inspirations, LLC
Huntsville, Alabama
tnhb.inspirations@yahoo.com
TNHB-Inspirations.com

Editorial Services - Voice Vessel Inspirations LLC
Cover Design courtesy of Fredrick Fluker, enfocus Media Group
Shannon Booker – Back Cover Photo Editor
Yvonne Rose/Qualitypress.info – Book Packager

All scripture references courtesy of (NLV) Bible
All quotes have been identified by author.

All Rights Reserved

No part of this book may be reproduced or transmitted in any form or by any means, unless permission is obtained by the author.

The content provided herein is for informational and inspirational purposes only and does not take place of any medical consultations.

Copyright © 2017 Travasa Buford
ISBN# 978-0-692-96515-3

DEDICATION

I dedicate this writing journey to Evelyn Peden.
My beloved grandmamma
Your spirit lives on through me

ACKNOWLEDGEMENTS

With gratitude, I thank God for not taking His hands off me when I wanted to let go. I realize the gift that I have to encourage others and I'm grateful for the angels that He has encompassed around me when I need an encouraging Word to get through my day. With Love, I thank you and I love you to life.

Ra'Mon & Rod Holloway
Pastor Rabon L. & Mia Turner
Pastor Tyshawn & Shonetay Gardner
Dr. Derrol & Patricia H. Dawkins
Pastor Leroy & Tina Caudle
Bishop Daniel J. & Tiffany Richardson
Minister Della Linwood
Randy & Demi Howell
Family & Friends

CONTENTS

Dedication --- i
Acknowledgements --- iii
Contents -- v
Preface -- xxi
Introduction -- xxiii

January 1 : You're Still Here -- 1
January 2 : Your Scars Will Soon Be Stars ---------------------------------- 2
January 3 : You've Earned Your Stripes ------------------------------------- 3
January 4 : Your Sorrow Will Turn Into Joy --------------------------------- 4
January 5 : Your Promise Is Coming --- 5
January 6 : Your Prayers Have Power -- 6
January 7 : You're Not A Quitter! -- 7
January 8 : You're Going To Make It Anyway --------------------------------- 8
January 9 : Your Pain Will Produce   Your Greatest Praise ------------------ 9
January 10 : Your Tears Are Collected -------------------------------------- 10
January 11 : You're Not Forgotten -- 11
January 12 : You're Not Built To Break ------------------------------------- 12
January 13 : Your Suffering Is Not In Vain --------------------------------- 13
January 14 : This Is Your Wake-Up Call ------------------------------------- 14
January 15 : Your Victory Is In Your Praise -------------------------------- 15
January 16 : Your Sacrifices Will Be Rewarded ------------------------------ 16
January 17 : I Can't Go Back To What Made Me Sick -------------------------- 17
January 18 : Your I.D. --- 18

January 19 : Your Enemy Will Not Triumph Over You! ---------------- 19

January 20 : You're Next In Line For A Miracle ------------------------- 20

January 21 : You're God's Child --- 21

January 22 : You Won't Stay Down --------------------------------------- 22

January 23 : You Will Win -- 23

January 24 : You Will Not Be Shaken ----------------------------------- 24

January 25 : You Will Get It Back --------------------------------------- 25

January 26 : You Will Cry No More ------------------------------------- 26

January 27 : You Were Made Stronger ---------------------------------- 27

January 28 : You Weren't Built To Break ------------------------------- 28

January 29 : You Still Got The Power ----------------------------------- 29

January 30 : You Might Know --- 30

January 31 : You Have To Go Through It ------------------------------ 31

February 1 : You Got This -- 32

February 2 : You Don't Need That Addiction...
But You Do Need The Word ------------------------------- 33

February 3 : You Don't Have To Stay There! --------------------------- 34

February 4 : You Can't, But God Can ----------------------------------- 35

February 5 : You Can't Stay Stuck There ------------------------------- 36

February 6 : You Can Get Through This -------------------------------- 37

February 7 : You Are -- 38

February 8 : You Are Victorious -- 39

February 9 : You Are Important To God -------------------------------- 40

February 10 : You Are Covered -- 41

February 11 : You Are Blessed --- 42

February 12 : You Are Anointed --- 43

February 13 : You Are A Soldier -- 44

February 14 : You Always Win -- 45

February 15 : You Already Won --- 46

February 16 : You Almost -- 47

February 17 : Yes….It Happened --- 48

February 18 : Wishy Washy --- 49

February 19 : Why You Keep Picking On Me? -------------------------- 50

February 20 : Why You Are Trying To Figure It Out?
                  When He Is Already Working It Out --------------------- 51

February 21 : Who Did You Tell? --- 52

February 22 : Who Are You Seeking -------------------------------------- 53

February 23 : When You Believe, God Works --------------------------- 54

February 24 : When It Doesn't Make Sense ------------------------------ 55

February 25 : When God Is In It -- 56

February 26 : Whatcha Gonna Do? --- 57

February 27 : What You Say? -- 58

February 28 : What It Caused --- 59

March 1 : You Can't Hide --- 60

March 2 : You Can't Break Now --- 61

March 3 : You Can't Be Silent --- 62

March 4 : What Did You Just Say? --- 63

March 5 : What Are You Looking At? -------------------------------------- 65

March 6 : Watch What I Can Do -- 66

March 7 : Walk Victoriously -- 67

March 8 : Walk Like You Already Know ----------------------------------- 68

March 9 : Walk By Faith -- 69

March 10 : Wake Up --- 70
March 11 : Waiting Time... Isn't Wasted Time --- 71
March 12 : Wait A Minute --- 72
March 13 : Victory Is Mine --- 73
March 14 : Turn Your Worry Into Worship --- 74
March 15 : Turn The Page --- 75
March 16 : Trust The Lord --- 76
March 17 : Trust His Process --- 77
March 18 : Trouble, Drama, & Trauma --- 78
March 19 : Trouble Don't Last Always --- 79
March 20 : Tragedy To Triumph --- 80
March 21 : Trade It --- 81
March 22 : Touch Not My Anointed --- 82
March 23 : Too Many Times --- 83
March 24 : Through It All You're Still Standing --- 84
March 25 : Defending A Lie --- 85
March 26 : This Is Your Season --- 86
March 27 : This Is My Promise To You --- 87
March 28 : This Is Just The Beginning --- 88
March 29 : This Is It --- 89
March 30 : This & That-That & This --- 90
March 31 : Think Like And Act Like A Winner --- 91

April 1 : They Said No, God Says Yes --- 92
April 2 : They Gotta Go --- 93
April 3 : They Can't Stand Me... But They Can't Stop Me --- 94

April 4 : They Better Watch It ---------- 95
April 5 : There Is A Reason For It ---------- 96
April 6 : The Truth Hurts ---------- 97
April 7 : The Sun & The Son ---------- 98
April 8 : The Struggle Is Real ---------- 99
April 9 : The Strength To Deal With It ---------- 100
April 10 : The Storm Is Over ---------- 101
April 11 : The Situation ---------- 102
April 12 : Too Strong To Let Them Tear You Down ---------- 103
April 13 : The Road To Victory ---------- 104
April 14 : The Question? ---------- 105
April 15 : The Process ---------- 106
April 16 : It Is Finished…He Has Risen ---------- 107
April 17 : The Pain Equals The Blessings ---------- 108
April 18 : The Original Gps ---------- 109
April 19 : The Next Thing Will Be The Best Thing ---------- 110
April 20 : The Lord Will Step Right In ---------- 111
April 21 : The Energizer Bunny ---------- 112
April 22 : The Lord Will Fight For You ---------- 113
April 23 : The Enemy Doesn't Play Fair ---------- 114
April 24 : The Devil Isn't In A Red Cape ---------- 115
April 25 : The Devil Has A Plot But God Has A Plan ---------- 116
April 26 : The Devil Didn't Destroy You ---------- 117
April 27 : The Desires Of Your Heart ---------- 118
April 28 : The Attack Will Come To An End ---------- 119
April 29 : Thank God For The Pressure ---------- 120
April 30 : Tell Yourself ---------- 121

May 1 : Talk Like You Know --- 122

May 2 : Taking Out The Trash --- 123

May 3 : Swing Batter Batter Swing --- 124

May 4 : Surrender --- 125

May 5 : Stuck --- 126

May 6 : Stronger, Better And Brighter --- 127

May 7 : Strength Within --- 128

May 8 : Stop! The Fear Is Gone --- 129

May 9 : Stop! Now Just Let God --- 130

May 10 : Sticks & Stones May Break My Bones...
  But God Reigns In Me --- 131

May 11 : Stick & Tough It Out --- 132

May 12 : Stepping Out --- 133

May 13 : Stepping Out On Faith --- 134

May 14 : Step --- 135

May 15 : Stay --- 136

May 16 : Stay Faithful --- 137

May 17 : Starting Over --- 138

May 18 : Stand Tall --- 139

May 19 : Stand Firm --- 140

May 20 : Stand Back Up --- 141

May 21 : So What --- 142

May 22 : Sit Back & Watch The Show --- 143

May 23 : Sick & Tired Of Being Sick & Tired --- 144

May 24 : Shut Up & Pray --- 146

May 25 : Show Up For God &   He Will Show Out For You --- 147

May 26 : Shout --- 148

May 27 : Shhhhhh & Listen --- 149
May 28 : Seek Him First --- 150
May 29 : You Got This --- 151
May 30 : See No Evil, Hear No Evil --- 152
May 31 : Run To God --- 153

June 1 : Rise Up --- 154
June 2 : Right On Time --- 155
June 3 : You Can't Fool A Seed --- 156
June 4 : Rejoicing, Restoration & Restitution --- 157
June 5 : Rejoice In Tribulation --- 158
June 6 : Rejoice Even When --- 159
June 7 : Redirected --- 160
June 8 : Recovery Time --- 161
June 9 : Quit Looking At The Negative --- 162
June 10 : Pushed Into Your Purpose --- 163
June 11 : Press, Push & Pray --- 164
June 12 : Press Harder --- 165
June 13 : Prayers & Patience = Blessings --- 166
June 14 : Prayer Will Change Your Situation --- 167
June 15 : Pray For Them --- 168
June 16 : Pray For Others Than Yourself --- 169
June 17 : Praise Until He Lets Go --- 170
June 18 : Praise Through The Pressure --- 171
June 19 : Praise In Pain --- 172
June 20 : Peace Be Still --- 173

June 21 : Overcoming --- 174
June 22 : Opponent = Victory --- 175
June 23 : One Day This Will Be Your Testimony --- 176
June 24 : Okay…It Happened --- 177
June 25 : Obey And Just Do It --- 178
June 26 : Now = Greater Later --- 179
June 27 : Notice Served: Eviction To The Enemy --- 180
June 28 : Not Your Way…But God's --- 181
June 29 : Not Today --- 182
June 30 : Not The End, But A New Beginning --- 183

July 1 : Not Destroyed --- 184
July 2 : Nobody Said The Road Would Be Easy --- 185
July 3 : Nobody Greater --- 186
July 4 : No Time To Be Weary Or Worried --- 187
July 5 : No Need To Beg --- 188
July 6 : No Need To Be Afraid --- 189
July 7 : No Evil For Evil --- 190
July 8 : Never Stop Praying --- 191
July 9 : Never Again --- 192
July 10 : Moving On --- 193
July 11 : Move Out Of The Way --- 194
July 12 : More Problems But Louder Praises --- 195
July 13 : Make God Famous --- 196
July14 : Lose To Win --- 197
July 15 : Lord, Help Me --- 198

July 16 : Look To God --- 199
July 17 : Little Or Great Faith? --- 200
July 18 : Let Your Light Shine --- 201
July 19 : Let Your Enemies Push You --- 202
July 20 : Let Them Walk --- 203
July 21 : Let Them Come --- 204
July 22 : Haters Can't Take Nothing From You --- 205
July 23 : Let It Train You --- 206
July 24 : Let God Work In Your Life --- 207
July 25 : Let God Take Care Of Them --- 208
July 26 : Let God See Your Faith --- 209
July 27 : Let God Pay Back --- 210
July 28 : Let God Do It --- 211
July 29 : Let God Deal With The Outcome --- 212
July 30 : Lean Not Unto Thy Own Understanding --- 213
July 31 : Know Who Is In Control --- 214

August 1 : Know Where Your Help Comes From --- 215
August 2 : Knock Knock --- 216
August 3 : Kneel --- 217
August 4 : Keep Smiling --- 218
August 5 : Keep Pushing --- 219
August 6 : Keep Praying Persistently --- 220
August 7 : Keep Praying & Stop Worrying --- 221
August 8 : Keep On Ticking --- 222
August 9 : Keep On Praising --- 223

August 10 : Keep On Keeping On -- 224
August 11 : Keep Looking To God--------------------------------------- 225
August 12 : Keep It Moving-- 226
August 13 : Keep Doing Your Part ------------------------------------- 227
August 14 : Just Say, Jesus! -- 228
August 15 : Judgement For: Pain & Suffering ------------------------- 229
August 16 : Jesus Made A Way For You ------------------------------- 230
August 17 : I've Never-- 231
August 18 : It's What You're Made Of ---------------------------------- 232
August 19 : It's Under Your Feet--------------------------------------- 233
August 20 : It's Time To Pray--- 234
August 21 : It's Revealing--- 235
August 22 : It's Raining --- 236
August 23 : It's Painful -- 237
August 24 : It's Out Of Control…But ---------------------------------- 238
August 25 : It's Not Over -- 239
August 26 : It's Not By Accident --------------------------------------- 240
August 27 : It's Not A Punishment------------------------------------- 241
August 28 : It's Necessary-- 242
August 29 : It's Just A Test --- 243
August 30 : It's Hot In Here--- 244
August 31 : It's His Will That You Face It ----------------------------- 245

September 1 : It's His Promise --- 246
September 2 : It's Handled --- 247
September 3 : It's Getting Rough -------------------------------------- 248

September 4 : It's For A Reason --------------------------------------- 249

September 5 : It's Called A Fiery Trial--------------------------------- 250

September 6 : It's Been Hard -- 251

September 7 : It's Already Done--------------------------------------- 252

September 8 : It's A Process -- 253

September 9 : It's A Moving Situation--------------------------------- 254

September 10 : It's A Battle --- 255

September 11 : It's Your Due Season ---------------------------------- 256

September 12 : It's The Worst--- 257

September 13 : It's The Joy You Have --------------------------------- 258

September 14 : It's Preparing You------------------------------------- 259

September 15 : It's Not Wasted --------------------------------------- 260

September 16 : It's Not Too Late ------------------------------------- 261

September 17 : It's Not That Serious --------------------------------- 262

September 18 : It's Not Impossible ----------------------------------- 263

September 19 : It's Not Fair--- 264

September 20 : It's Not An Option ----------------------------------- 265

September 21 : It's Happening For A Reason------------------------- 266

September 22 : It's Got To Get Deep --------------------------------- 267

September 23 : It's Going To Make You Stronger--------------------- 268

September 24 : It's Going To Be Ok ---------------------------------- 269

September 25 : It's Getting Rough ------------------------------------ 270

September 26 : It's Behind You, Now Look Ahead -------------------- 271

September 27 : It's Always Something -------------------------------- 272

September 28 : It's All Good -- 273

September 29 : It's All Good -- 274

September 30 : It's About Where You Are Going --------------------- 275

October 1 : It's A Spiritual Thang --- 276
October 2 : It Won't Rain Forever --- 277
October 3 : It Won't Last --- 278
October 4 : It Won't Be Me --- 279
October 5 : It Was Disappointing --- 280
October 6 : It Taught You --- 281
October 7 : It Takes One Step --- 282
October 6 : It Will Work Out --- 283
October 7 : The Power Of God Is In You --- 284
October 8 : It Happened --- 285
October 9 : It Had To Get Real --- 286
October 10 : It Had To Get Messy --- 287
October 11 : It Formed, But --- 288
October 12 : It Doesn't Look Good --- 289
October 13 : It Didn't Break You --- 290
October 14 : It Could Be Worse --- 291
October 15 : It Can Come Up Missing --- 292
October 16 : It Ain't Over, Until God Says It --- 293
October 17 : Is Fear Ruling You? --- 294
October 18 : Intimidate Your Intimidator(S)   With Praise --- 295
October 19 : Insane Faith --- 296
October 20 : In The Storm --- 297
October 21 : In The End...You Win --- 298
October 22 : In His Hands --- 299
October 23 : In God's Timing --- 300
October 24 : In Due Time --- 301
October 25 : I'm A Giant Killer --- 302

October 26 : If You Are Concerned About It... He Cares About It --- 303

October 27 : If He Did It Before He Can Do It Again --- 304

October 28 : If God Can Hear You He Will Heal You --- 305

October 29 : I Will Fear No Evil --- 306

October 30 : I Want What I Want --- 307

October 31 : I Need To Be --- 308

November 1 : I Have To --- 309

November 2 : I Got The Power --- 310

November 3 : I Don't Feel Like It --- 311

November 4 : Hurt But Not Broken --- 312

November 5 : How Big Is It? --- 313

November 6 : Hold Your Peace --- 314

November 7 : Hold On To God's Unchanging Hand --- 315

November 8 : Hold On A Lil While Longer --- 316

November 9 : Hit Hard --- 317

November 10 : His Power Can Get You Through --- 318

November 11 : His Light Is Still Shining --- 319

November 12 : He'll Pick You Back Up --- 320

November 13 : Heels High....Heads High --- 321

November 14 : He's Working --- 322

November 15 : He Will Raise You Up --- 323

November 16 : He Will End Your Suffering --- 324

November 17 : He Will Always Provide --- 325

November 18 : He Will Accomplish His Purpose And Promises --- 326

November 19 : He Used It --- 327

November 20 : He Sees, Hears And Will Deliver --- 328
November 21 : He Saves The Best For Last --- 329
November 22 : He Will Restore You --- 330
November 23 : Thankful --- 331
November 24 : He Keeps His Hands On You --- 332
November 25 : He Is --- 333
November 26 : He Is Strengthening You --- 334
November 27 : He Reigns --- 335
November 28 : He Is Still Worthy --- 336
November 29 : He Is Still Good --- 337
November 30 : He Is Always On Time --- 338

December 1 : Have A Little Faith --- 339
December 2 : Greater --- 340
December 3 : Greater Is Coming --- 341
December 4 : Great Is His Faithfulness --- 342
December 5 : Got Problems... Get More Praises --- 343
December 6 : Got Faith? --- 344
December 7 : God's Delays Are Not His Denials --- 345
December 8 : God Will Work It Out --- 346
December 9 : God Will Sustain You --- 347
December 10 : God Will Supply --- 348
December 11 : God Will Step In The Situation --- 349
December 12 : God Puts People In Your Life For A Reason --- 350
December 13 : God Is Turning It Around --- 351
December 14 : Every Little Step You Take --- 352

December 15 : Fight Fixed — 353
December 16 : Get On Up — 354
December 17 : Expect It! — 355
December 18 : Even When In Doubt — 356
December 19 : Don't Stop Believing — 357
December 20 : Don't Get Stuck In The Moment — 358
December 21 : Better Days Are Coming — 359
December 22 : Be Strong While You Wait — 360
December 23 : A Peace Of Mind Is Priceless — 361
December 24 : A Christmas Miracle — 362
December 25 : Beyond The Lights — 363
December 26 : Amazing Grace — 364
December 27 : A Hundredfold Return — 365
December 28 : A Masterpiece — 366
December 29 : A Blessing In Every Lesson — 367
December 30 : A Mistake Or A Decision — 368
December 31 : A Battle Turned Into A Blessing — 369
About The Author — 371

PREFACE

What do you do when life throws you some unexpected blows and you are shook to your very core? Do you crawl into a fetal position and remain there as life passes you by? Do you shut your eyes and hope this turbulent dark storm will just end? **At The End of the Day**, embodies the faith and resilience of this Author's work as she wrote from a place of bitter brokenness, which later blossomed into her courageous gift and beauty. The author began sharing her daily devotionals with her readers electronically through TNHB Inspirations. Once, her readers connected with her and responded, she understood that her writing had to continue. The author understood that there were others waiting to be reminded that, though life may knock you down, At the End of the Day, You Won't Stay Down. In fact, you will arise from that fetal position and take your life back. You will open your eyes and face the storm head on and ride the wind to your next destination. **At the End of the Day**, I hope you always choose to ride the wind to your next destination.

- Shannon B. Talley
Author, Hear My Voice and Committing Suicide to Live Again
Voice Vessel Inspirations LLC

INTRODUCTION

Misused Abused Disrespected Battered Weary Hurt Embarrassed Broken Lost Depressed Suicidal

She was living in hell, now she is in a haven, a refuge, protected, covered, and she is no longer bound. She is pressing forward with the confidence in knowing that no weapon formed shall prosper. She no longer is allowing Man's rejection to define her. The moment she was rejected, God re-directed, promoted and protected her. She has finally released the imprisonment of the past grudges, anger and resentment. She has let go of the poisonous venom of the past that has haunted her. She fell, she crashed, she broke, she cried, she crawled, she hurt, she surrendered, and then she rose again...

I Am Travasa Natasha Holloway Buford of TNHB Inspirations, LLC.

I'd like to encourage you to journal your own thoughts after each devotion with your own *At The End OF The Day* reflection. May your entire year be filled with peace, love, and joy. May you always know that *At The End Of The Day*, no matter where you fall in life, You shall rise again.

Sincerely,
Travasa

JANUARY 1

YOU'RE STILL HERE

Despite what has happened to you, you're still standing. God has made you like a tree planted by the water that sends out its roots by the stream. It does not fear when heat comes; its leaves are always green. It has no worries in a year of drought and never fails to bear fruit. (Jeremiah 17:8)

Today know that God is patient with you and is not slow to fulfill His promises for your life. The devil is not going to take you out. (2 Peter 3:9)

That person is like a tree planted by streams of water, which yields its fruit in season and whose leaf does not wither, whatever they do prospers. (Psalm 1:3)

Remember, you've had your share of heartache, pain, setback and even trouble; BUT you're still here!

At the end of the day:

_____
_____
_____
_____
_____
_____
_____
_____
_____

JANUARY 2

YOUR SCARS WILL SOON BE STARS

I know the hurricane and tornado that you are dealing with is too much to bear. The scars might be physically there but God is getting ready to give you stars for all of the wrong that has been done in your life. All you have to do is trust Him! Surrender it all over to Him and watch Him move on your behalf.

Today, think of yourself as playing in the NBA and you're in pain but you are in the final quarter with: 30 seconds left on the clock and the game is tied and the opponent has the ball, but just fouled. Well that's a shout queue for someone today to know that you might be in pain, it might hurt, you might be able to see the scars, but it isn't over till God says so!

His master replied, "Well done, good and faithful servant! You have been faithful with a few things; I will put you in charge of many things. Come and share your master's happiness!" Remember, stay in the game. God is going to take care of the rest! (Matthew 25:21)

At the end of the day:

_____
_____
_____
_____
_____
_____
_____
_____

JANUARY 3

YOU'VE EARNED YOUR STRIPES

The storms that you have gone through didn't sweep you away. But what they did do is make you unmovable, showing that God can give his toughest battles to His strongest soldiers.

Today, look at the situation like you're a tiger and have earned every stripe you carry. There is nothing about you that says you are a victim, but a victor that can weather through the hardest battles of your life!

Remember, mothers often times get stretch marks as a result of giving birth. See, God places seeds for us to birth something out. When it's over you have something beautiful to share with the world. The marks on you are just proof that you earned your stripes!

But he was wounded for our transgressions; he was bruised for our iniquities: the chastisement of our peace was upon him; and with his stripes we are healed. (Isaiah 53:5)

Stay Prayed Up & Encouraged

At the end of the day:

_____
_____
_____
_____
_____
_____
_____
_____

JANUARY 4

YOUR SORROW WILL TURN INTO JOY

Today is your day for restoration and healing. I know you have been in some trying times lately. Pillow soaked of tears, and a heart full of worry. You are literally all cried out. Praying day and night and still nothing! You sit and ponder the question, "Why God?"

Your sorrow is getting ready to turn into joy. God has seen how you have been faithful over a few things and now He is getting ready to flood you with many. (Matthew 25:21) When a woman is giving birth, she has sorrow because her hour has come, but when she has delivered the baby, she no longer remembers the anguish, for joy that a human being has been born into the world. (John 16:21)

This is God's new birth and blessings for your life! Get Ready!

I am acting with great boldness toward you; I have great pride in you; I am filled with comfort. In all our affliction, I am overflowing with joy. (2 Corinthians 7:4)

At the end of the day:

_____
_____
_____
_____
_____
_____
_____
_____
_____

JANUARY 5

YOUR PROMISE IS COMING

Has God spoken things to your heart that haven't come to pass yet? Sometimes when we believe for things to come in our lives that we have been praying for and it is taking longer...well we get impatient, aggravated and uneasy. But you have to make the choice to receive God's promise and start to picture it in your mind and see it. You must declare and decree a thing into existence!

Today, have joy and peace so you can begin to feel more confident and more settled on the inside. God is working behind the scenes on your behalf. Open your heart and allow God's thoughts to become your thoughts and receive His promises by Faith. He will do EXACTLY what He said He will do!

Therefore, I tell you, whatever you ask for in prayer, believe that you have received it, and it will be yours. (Mark 11:24)

At the end of the day:

_____
_____
_____
_____
_____
_____
_____
_____
_____
_____

JANUARY 6

YOUR PRAYERS HAVE POWER

When you are going through it, it is easy to sit back and talk about what your circumstances and problems are, but the reality is what good is that going to do? If you really want to see your situation change, you are going to have to give it over to The Lord and pray about it. (Philippians 4:6)

Whatever you ask in prayer, believe that you have received it, and it will be yours. (Mark 11:24)

Remember, the prayers of a righteous person are powerful and effective. (James 5:16)

Today you need to know that there is power when you pray to God.

Whatever you ask in my name, this I will do, that the Father may be glorified in the Son. If you ask me anything in my name, I will do it. (John 14:13-14)

At the end of the day:

_____
_____
_____
_____
_____
_____
_____
_____

JANUARY 7

YOU'RE NOT A QUITTER!

When you're enduring a storm it's easy to just want to throw in the towel and give up…but that's what the enemy is counting on. Right now, declare and decree that you are not a quitter, but a winner!

Today, tell Satan he can go back to where he came from. No matter what he throws at you, keep on ducking, diving and dodging from his evil tricks. He can't have you because God's hand is on your life.

Remember, winners never quit and quitters never win!

Stay Prayed up and Encouraged

But as for you, be strong and do not give up, for your work will be rewarded. (2 Chronicles 15:7)

At the end of the day:

_____
_____
_____
_____
_____
_____
_____
_____
_____
_____
_____
_____
_____

JANUARY 8

YOU'RE GOING TO MAKE IT ANYWAY

If you had to look back in the rear-view mirror of your life; you probably would have thought then, that you wouldn't have made it this far. But thank God for His grace!

Today give God praise because despite how many times the enemy tried to take you out.... The good Lord was right there shielding and protecting you.

Remember, the next time you feel an attack from the devil. Tell him, You tried, but I'm still here and I'm going to make it anyway.

You, dear children, are from God and have overcome them, because the one who is in you is greater than the one who is in the world. (1 John 4:4)

At the end of the day:

_____
_____
_____
_____
_____
_____
_____
_____
_____
_____
_____

JANUARY 9

YOUR PAIN WILL PRODUCE YOUR GREATEST PRAISE

I know it is hard to keep pressing and moving forward when you're hurt, broken and in pain. You must know that God wants you to not only praise HIM when times are good but, He also wants you to praise HIM when times are bad.... And when you hurt the most.

Today rejoice in your suffering, problems and trials for they will develop your endurance. (Romans 5:3) Hold your head up and be glad, for these trials make you partners with Christ in his suffering, so that you will have the wonderful joy of seeing His glory when it is revealed. (1 Peter 4:13)

Remember; count it all joy when you meet trials of various kinds. Know that the testing of your faith produces steadfastness; and let steadfastness have its full effect. So that you may be perfect and complete and lack in nothing. (James 1:2-4)

That's why I take pleasure in my weaknesses and in the insults, hardships, persecutions, and troubles that I suffer for Christ. For when I am weak, then I am strong. (2 Corinthians 12:10)

At the end of the day:

_____
_____
_____
_____
_____
_____
_____

JANUARY 10

YOUR TEARS ARE COLLECTED

All of us are important to God. He cares about every single thing that we are going through. Don't get dismayed or discouraged because you think the pillow soaked full of tears last night went unnoticed. God heard your cries and He knows why you are crying. Not only did He hear them but He records every sorrow that you are going through and has collected every teardrop.

Today, hold your head up high and know that although you cried last night and you feel overwhelmed with the circumstances that you are going through. Know that God is with you all the way. Not one tear you shed will He not pick up.

He is bringing Restoration and Healing to your Soul.

You keep track of all my sorrows. You have collected all my tears in your bottle. You have recorded each one in your book. (Psalm 56:8)

At the end of the day:

_____
_____
_____
_____
_____
_____
_____
_____
_____

JANUARY 11

YOU'RE NOT FORGOTTEN

It might seem that you are in your home or apartment all alone in the natural; but my dear friend you are never alone.

Today, just because it might feel like the waves of the storms are taking you under. God is with you the whole time. Every tear you have shed, every scream you've let out and every pace you've walked. He's been right there.

Remember, through it all God is with you. Holding, Comforting and Protecting You.

He has not forgotten about YOU!

Stay Prayed Up & Encouraged

Don't be afraid, for I am with you. Don't be discouraged, for I am your God. I will strengthen you and help you. I will hold you up with my victorious right hand. For I hold you by your right hand... I, the LORD your God. And I say to you, "Don't be afraid. I am here to help you." (Isaiah 41:10, 13)

At the end of the day:

_____
_____
_____
_____
_____
_____

JANUARY 12

YOU'RE NOT BUILT TO BREAK

Everything that you are going through might have you feeling like you are about to crumble, but God won't let that happen. He has chosen the foolish things of the world to shame the wise, and has chosen the weak things of the world to shame the things which are strong. (1 Corinthians 1:27)

Today don't focus on your circumstances and don't look at the odds against you. Instead keep your eyes on the prize and press forward. (Philippians 3:14)

Remember, you're not built to break!

The Lord is keeping you from all harm and watching over your life. (Psalm 121:7)

There shall be a time of trouble; such as there never has been since there was a nation... till that time. But at that time your people shall be delivered, everyone whose name shall be found written in the book. (Daniel 12:1)

At the end of the day:

_____
_____
_____
_____
_____
_____
_____
_____

JANUARY 13

YOUR SUFFERING IS NOT IN VAIN

I wish I could tell you that you're not going to endure any suffering and hardships in this world. But the fact is when you are a soldier for Christ; you can expect hardships and sufferings to increase in your life. So, you must be armed, prepared and ready for battle. (2 Tim. 2:3)

Today, no matter what has got you stuck in bed, depressed, crying and suicidal. Tell the devil that you are aware of his schemes!!!!! (2 Corinthians 2:11) Rejoice while you are suffering now, and know that it is while you are going through that, this is going to produce endurance, character and hope! (Romans 5:3-4)

Remember, after you have suffered a little while, the God of all grace, who has called you to His eternal glory in Christ, will Himself restore, confirm, strengthen, and establish you! (1 Peter 5:10)

Count it all joy, my brothers, when you meet trials of various kinds, for you know that the testing of your faith produces steadfastness. And let steadfastness have its full effect, that you may be perfect and complete, lacking in nothing. (James 1:2-4)

At the end of the day:

_____
_____
_____
_____
_____
_____
_____

JANUARY 14

THIS IS YOUR WAKE-UP CALL

There comes a time that we have to realize that WE ALL are going to have to be held accountable for our actions on this earth! How you treat people, how you're living, the things you're doing...HE SEES EVERYTHING! This is YOUR wake-up call. I don't know what is going on in your life; but I know the things that I'm doing that I've had to check myself on and ask God forgiveness on. I pray that you can recognize the things that you know that are ugly and not of God and change your ways as well. We all should want to hear, "Well done, thy faithful servant, Well Done!"

Nothing in all creation is hidden from God. Everything is naked and exposed before his eyes, and he is the one to whom we are accountable. (Hebrews 4:13)

At the end of the day:

_____
_____
_____
_____
_____
_____
_____
_____
_____
_____
_____

JANUARY 15

YOUR VICTORY IS IN YOUR PRAISE

God has done some wonderful things. Accomplishing plans He formed long ago made with perfect faithfulness. For He is our God, Our Lord and deserves to be lifted in praise. (Isaiah 25:1)

Everybody in this world is dealing with something. Whether it is small, big or major we are going through something. Instead of complaining about it, we should continually offer up a sacrifice of praise to God and acknowledge His name. (Hebrews 13:15)

Today, this week and every day moving forward, give thanks to the Lord, for He is good; for His steadfast love endures forever. (Psalm 118:29) Know that there is nothing that we are going through that is too hard for God to fix. For He has kept and is keeping us now; and will continue to watch over us. (Psalm 121:7)

Remember, God is not attracted to your problems, but He is attracted to your praise!

Therefore, I will praise you, Lord, among the nations; I will sing the praises of your name. (2 Samuel 22:50)

At the end of the day:

_____
_____
_____
_____
_____
_____
_____

JANUARY 16

YOUR SACRIFICES WILL BE REWARDED

You may have made sacrifices in your life, marriage, and career and even as a parent. Sometimes it can be hard when you look at things in the natural and it's seems like you're dealing with an unfair situation.

Today, know that God rewards those who are faithful. He will lift your head above your enemies and shouts of joy will come from your mouth; and you will know it was God and God only! (Psalm 27:6)

Remember; be strong and courageous, for your work will be rewarded. (2 Chronicles 15:7)

Whatever you do, work heartily, as for the Lord and not for men, knowing that from the Lord you will receive the inheritance as your reward. You are serving the Lord Christ. (Colossians 3:23-24)

At the end of the day:

_____
_____
_____
_____
_____
_____
_____
_____
_____
_____
_____

JANUARY 17

I CAN'T GO BACK TO WHAT MADE ME SICK

Have you ever been in a situation that was so bad that it made you physically and mentally sick? But you loved it. Tina told Ike," What's Love Got To Do With it?"

I love strawberries but I'm also allergic to them. So eating them will cause me to go into anaphylactic shock. Therefore, I don't eat them. So stop running back to what makes you sick!

Remember, just like a dog that returns to its vomit, Is a fool who repeats his foolishness. Proverbs 26:11

Throw off your old sinful nature and your former way of life, which is corrupted by lust and deception. Ephesians 4:22

At the end of the day:

___
___
___
___
___
___
___
___
___
___
___
___
___
___

JANUARY 18

YOUR I.D.

The things that have occurred to you are not your identity. You can't let the failures, divorce, heartbreak, pain, breakup, bankruptcy and the addiction define who you are. None of those things change the fact that you are still a child of the most High God.

Today, realize that you might have had some setbacks and folks probably spoke negative things about you; but count it all joy because at the end of the day, "they" don't determine your destiny. You are who God says you are.

Remember, let go and get rid of the excuses and negativity. You are equipped, empowered and more than a conqueror. Your destiny will be fulfilled!

The Lord will work out his plans for my life for your faithful love, O Lord, endures forever. Don't abandon me, for you made me. (Psalm 138:8)

At the end of the day:

_____
_____
_____
_____
_____
_____
_____
_____

JANUARY 19

YOUR ENEMY WILL NOT TRIUMPH OVER YOU!

Things might have been hard for you these past months/year. No one even knows the tears you've cried or the pain and hurt that you've felt inside. But thanks, be to God who calls us to triumph in Christ!!! (2 Corinthians 2:14)

Today, count it all joy for the trouble, trials and storms that have come your way. It taught you to know where your help comes from and where to lean on; and as hard as they tried... your enemies will not triumph over you!!! (Psalm 25:2)

Remember, you can't even believe or begin to fathom the great wonders of this world that God has for those who love him! (1 Corinthians 2:9)

Stay Prayed Up & Encouraged

He rescued me from my powerful enemies, from those who hated me and were too strong for me. (Psalm 18:17)

At the end of the day:

_____
_____
_____
_____
_____
_____
_____
_____

JANUARY 20

YOU'RE NEXT IN LINE FOR A MIRACLE

It's easy to get discouraged and get heartbroken when you're wanting, expecting and needing God to work in your life like only He can. The devil stays busy...so get ahead of him and put your spiritual armor on so you can defeat him before he attempts to come for you.

I don't care what they told you! When I tell you "they" no matter who it is ultimately, your "they "is really the devil!

Whether "they" said: "I don't want you, We're not hiring at this time, You will never be anything, I don't like you, This job isn't for you, Your too fat, Your credit is too low, You need a college degree, Get out of my house, You're fired, You're not good enough, I want a divorce, You will never be able to do that."

I don't care what the devil has or is telling you.... Keep the Faith!

Today open your eyes and heart and walk by Faith and not by sight and believe with everything in you that you are a child of the High Most God and ALL of the riches and glory out here belong to him. "They" can tell you what they want to tell you, but thank God, WE know a higher power that will do the exceedingly and abundantly above all that we can ask, think, or imagine...because if you didn't know, well let me tell you...greater is He that is in YOU & ME than HE that is in the world!!!! (1 John 4:4)

Today is your day! You better walk like your miracle was just given to you on a silver platter by a butler, hand chosen by our Heavenly Father just for YOU only!

The Lord is not slow to fulfill his promise as some count slowness, but is patient toward you, not wishing that any should perish, but that all should reach repentance. (2 Peter 3:9)

At the end of the day:

JANUARY 21

YOU'RE GOD'S CHILD

It is such a blessing and wonderful feeling when you just sit back and think what it means to be a child of our Heavenly Father. No matter what we have done He still loves us. Even when things in life get tough and you feel alone, God is always right there with you by your side.

Because we are His children, we are privileged! He is always with us to help guide, teach, comfort, and give us peace, joy and strength when needed. Who else can give you grace, love, and provision when you need it? James 1:5 says If any of you lacks wisdom, you should ask God, who gives generously to all without finding fault, and it will be given to you. There is no other like Him!

Remember this- You are a Child of God, and He is able to meet you at your point of need. He is sufficient for you in good times and in bad times. He will always be your strength, even when you don't have the strength to keep pushing. If some days it feels that He is all you have, rest assured knowing He is all you need.

See what great love the Father has lavished on us, that we should be called children of God! And that is what we are! The reason the world does not know us is that it did not know him." (1 John 3:1)

Do not be anxious about anything, but in every situation, by prayer and petition, with thanksgiving, present your requests to God. And the peace of God, which transcends all understanding, will guard your hearts and your minds in Christ Jesus. (Philippians 4:6, 7)

At the end of the day:

_____

_____

_____

JANUARY 22

YOU WON'T STAY DOWN

Today you need to know that you may have been knocked down and let down... but brother and sister... the good Lord won't let you stay down.

God will not let you suffer and endure without providing a way out. Life happens. But we know that God doesn't give us more than we can bear. There is nothing that you are going through that God can't get you through. He is faithful!

(1 Corinthians 10:13) You must know that failure doesn't come from falling down. Failure comes from not getting back up.

Remember, sometimes you have to get knocked down lower than you have ever been, to stand back up taller than you ever were.

Though a righteous man falls seven times, he will get up, but the wicked will stumble into ruin. (Proverbs 24:16)

At the end of the day:

_____
_____
_____
_____
_____
_____
_____
_____
_____
_____
_____

JANUARY 23

YOU WILL WIN

I know what you are going through and you think no one can possibly understand how you feel or can begin to fathom your situation, but God says, "Weeping may endure for a night but Joy does come in the morning." (Psalm 30:5) In the carnal it might look like your "Goliath" is winning but we all know is how the story ends. (1 Samuel 17)

No matter what you are facing today, take confidence in knowing that, if you have a relationship with The Father, EVERYTHING works together for the good of those who love Him. (Romans 8:28)

You are more than a conqueror and God has already called the fight and declared you the winner. (Romans 8:37)

But thanks be to God, who gives us the victory through our Lord Jesus Christ. (1 Corinthians 15:57)

At the end of the day:

_____
_____
_____
_____
_____
_____
_____
_____
_____

JANUARY 24

YOU WILL NOT BE SHAKEN

Although raging storms can come flooding in your life you will remain like a tree, planted by the water that sends out its roots by the stream. There is no need to fear when the fire and heat come for you, because your leaves will remain green. Even in the drought, you will always bear fruit! (Jeremiah 17:8)

Today, don't let the enemy shake you off your game. You will not fall because you trust in Him and He is here to save you. (Jeremiah 39:18)

That person is like a tree planted by streams of water, which yields its fruit in season and whose leaf does not wither whatever they do prospers. (Psalm 1:3)

At the end of the day:

JANUARY 25

YOU WILL GET IT BACK

Today, know that God has called you a winner and everything that the enemy tried and did take; declare and decree right now that God will and is giving it all back. And it will be bigger, and better than ever before!

Remember God's servant Job? He lost it all and still kept the faith and trusted God. (Job 1:13-22) Just know that God will never leave you empty and with nothing. He is going to replace everything that you lost. What the enemy means for evil, God will work out for your good. (Genesis 50:20) I know it's been hard and every time you turn around it seems like you are losing and things are being taken from you. Loss, loss and more loss is all you seem to know...BUT THE DEVIL IS A LIE!

Hold on...Greater is Coming!!

At the end of the day:

JANUARY 26

YOU WILL CRY NO MORE

I know that you have cried so much that you feel like you can't even cry anymore. You feel hurt, embarrassed and ashamed. You don't want anyone to even see you shed another tear. But has anyone ever told you that Jesus wept? (John 11:35)

Today, I want you to rest assured and find comfort, although it looks bad. You have people telling you that it is not going to work out. The doctor is giving you a bad medical report as if he is God. Then your lawyer is giving you bad news as if the judge has already ruled in the case. Well, I am here to let you know that I don't care what "they" said. God will always have the last word! For we know the plans that He has for us to give us a future and a hope. (Jeremiah 29:11) Don't get discouraged, fret and weary over evil doers. (Psalm 37:1) Let God handle them. TRUST, He will handle them too. Weeping may endure for a night, brothers and sisters, but I promise you there WILL BE joy in the morning. (Psalm 30:5) Hold on! Your help is on the way.

He will wipe away every tear from their eyes, and death shall be no more, neither shall there be mourning, nor crying, nor pain anymore, for the former things have passed away. (Revelation 21:4)

At the end of the day:

_____
_____
_____
_____
_____
_____
_____

JANUARY 27

YOU WERE MADE STRONGER

Never take for granted how far God has brought you, If you looked back in the rearview mirror of your life; how can you not thank Him for bringing you this far?

Today, count it all joy for the pain, hurt, anguish, misery and difficulties that you have had to endure. Because your faith was just being tested and your endurance had a chance to grow. (James 1:3) (That's a shout que right there for many of you)

Remember, don't let life's troubles get you bitter and down. Instead let them make you better. You have become stronger because of your past and your testimony will be a blessing to someone else.

Stand firm, and you will win life. (Luke 21:19)

Blessed is the one who perseveres under trial because, having stood the test, that person will receive the crown of life that the Lord has promised to those who love him. (James 1:12)

At the end of the day:

_____
_____
_____
_____
_____
_____
_____
_____

JANUARY 28

YOU WEREN'T BUILT TO BREAK

God has given you every tool that you will need to make it in this life. It's the Bible! No matter what you are going through or how difficult you think your situation is, God IS going to see you through. You might be saying, "My situation is this or that."

Well here is the thing, God already knows what your situation is and He knew it before you stepped in it. He hasn't made you to live in poverty or have nothing in this life. God wants you to have all the riches and glory in the world. Peace, joy, love and happiness you will have. Every desire in your heart, He will bless you with it. (Psalm 37:4) But you have to have Faith!

Remember, Faith without work is dead. (James 2:14) So today step out on Faith and trust and tell Him what you need and give Him the praise and worship that He deserves. And I promise you He will start to move Heaven and Earth on your behalf!

And without faith, it is impossible to please him, for whoever would draw near to God must believe that He exists and that He rewards those who seek Him." (Hebrews 11:6)

At the end of the day:

_____
_____
_____
_____
_____
_____

JANUARY 29

YOU STILL GOT THE POWER

The devil comes to kill and destroy. (John 10:10) He will do anything and everything he can to take you down. It is imperative that you stay alert and have a sober mind. 1 Peter 5:8

Today, don't talk and walk as if you are defeated. In case you don't know, let me tell you. YOU ARE GOD'S CHILD!! You have already won the victory!! The battle and the storm that you THINK has caused you to go under, is really a sign that your blessing is right around the corner. God is getting ready to overflow your life like you have never seen before.

Remember, He gives his toughest assignments to His strongest soldiers. You are a SOLIDER!!! You can handle this because God has given you the power to come out victorious in it!

Show the devil who really has the power!

For God hath not given us the spirit of fear; but of power, and of love, and of a sound mind. 2 Timothy 1:7

At the end of the day:

_____

_____

_____

_____

_____

_____

_____

JANUARY 30

YOU MIGHT KNOW

You might know what it is like to have to rob Peter to pay Paul, and eat Ramen noodles for days because that's all you can afford. You might know what it is like to walk for miles to get to and from work or rolling pennies to get gas. You might know what it is like to have life taken from you... from the one you love.

Today you might know what it is like to experience the deepest level of pain, heartache and hell. But you can believe that it won't always be like this!!

Remember, telling yourself, "It Won't Always Be like This," is having faith. But telling The Lord to help me to benefit from this... will give you growth! (Denzel Hurd)

At the end of the day:

_____
_____
_____
_____
_____
_____
_____
_____
_____
_____
_____

JANUARY 31

YOU HAVE TO GO THROUGH IT

Many times when you are going through the enemy will creep up on you to make you feel as if you need to go ahead and throw in the towel. But the devil is a lie!!!

I know what is going on for you is not fair. I know that if anyone needs a breakthrough right now, it is YOU. But today I need you to take the thoughts of the enemy and throw them in the trash where they belong. You are just like Joseph in the Bible, and God is about to turn this thing around for you, but you have to go through it.

Remember, if Joseph had not been wrongfully thrown into prison he would have never interpreted the dreams that ultimately landed him to be ruler of a whole land. What you are going through is not in vain. If you will be faithful a little longer you will see what God will make you ruler of.

Hold on...It's almost over!

Yet what we suffer now is nothing compared to the glory he will reveal to us later. (Romans 8:18)

Now, Joseph was governor over the land. He was the one who sold to all the people of the land. And Joseph's brothers came and bowed themselves before him with their faces to the ground. (Genesis 42:6)

At the end of the day:

_____
_____
_____
_____

FEBRUARY 1

YOU GOT THIS

There is nothing going on in your life that is too hard for God. There may be days where you don't want to get out of bed and there are those days where you just cry out to God and say, "Lord please I just can't take no more!" But through it all, He has kept you from all harm and watched over your life. (Psalm 121:7)

Today, know that God has and will always keep a hedge of protection around you and your home. God will make you prosper in everything you do. (Job 1:10)

STOP WORRYING! YOU can do ALL things in Christ who strengthens you! (Philippians 4:13)

The LORD himself watches over you! The LORD stands beside you as your protective shade." (Psalm 121:5)

At the end of the day:

_____
_____
_____
_____
_____
_____
_____
_____
_____
_____

FEBRUARY 2

YOU DON'T NEED THAT ADDICTION... BUT YOU DO NEED THE WORD FROM GOD

It is easy to get caught up and let a doctor tell you that you need this pill and that pill to help you sleep at night and to make it through the day. Before you know it, you are walking dead, high on pills and sometimes even alcohol; completely addicted and letting that be your source of relief. No temptation has overtaken you that is not common to man. You need to know that God is faithful and He will not let you be tempted beyond your ability, but while you are tempted He will also provide a way of escape for you so that you may be able to endure it. (1 Corinthians 10:13)

Today, put everything down that you know you have become addicted to in your life. They are nothing but addictions that have become a war against your soul. (1 Peter 2:11) YOU DON'T NEED IT, but what you do need is a Word from God to get you through.

Blessed is the man who remains steadfast under trial, for when he has stood the test he will receive the crown of life, which God has promised to those who love Him. Let no one say when he is tempted, "I am being tempted by God," for God cannot be tempted with evil, and he himself tempts no one. But each person is tempted when he is lured and enticed by his own desire. Then, desire when it has conceived gives birth to sin; and sin, when it is fully grown brings forth death. (James 1:12-15)

At the end of the day:

_____
_____
_____
_____

FEBRUARY 3

YOU DON'T HAVE TO STAY THERE!

You may have fallen. You may have lost some things and some people may have left your side or life. Let those things go!!! God has told us in 1 John 2:19, "for if they had belonged to us, they would have remained with us."

Today, it's time to let it go and stop remaining in the pain, hurt and regret. You don't have to stay there. God has a blessing with your name on it and you can't receive it if you are stuck in the past. Life does go on and it is time to move on.

Remember, life is like a long highway. There will be many bumps along the way and road blocks you must maneuver through; but through it all you have to keep going.

So, keep the faith and keep pressing.... this too shall pass!

The righteous keep moving forward, and those with clean hands become stronger and stronger. (Job 17:9)

At the end of the day:

_____
_____
_____
_____
_____
_____
_____

FEBRUARY 4

YOU CAN'T, BUT GOD CAN

There may be a situation that you are facing where you know you have done everything you can to try to fix it. You have to realize that it is time to take "you" out of the equation and put God there.

Today, no matter what you are going through or what may be knocking at your door; you can't do it, but God can. And He can do exceeding abundantly above all that we ask or think, according to the power that works in us.

Remember, God is not a man, so He does not lie. There is not a promise that He will not fulfill. If He has said it, He will do it. (Numbers 23:19)

So, God has given both his promise and his oath. These two things are unchangeable because it is impossible for God to lie. Therefore, we who have fled to Him for refuge can have great confidence as we hold to the hope that lies before us. (Hebrews 6:18)

You can't, But God can and He Promised!!

At the end of the day:

_____
_____
_____
_____
_____
_____
_____
_____

FEBRUARY 5

YOU CAN'T STAY STUCK THERE

What you are going through is real. As young kids say, "The Struggle is Real." It's hard and if you talk about it...it may make you cry. But the good news is.... God won't let you stay there!

Today recognize that it does hurt and it doesn't feel good.... but God loves you too much to leave you in the pain, heartache and despair.

Remember, you will not stay in the hurt forever. So, don't get stuck with stuck people who want to see you stuck in tribulation. God is elevating YOU!

"Do not weep any longer, for I will reward you," says the LORD. (Jeremiah 31:16)

They will come with weeping; they will pray as I bring them back. I will lead them beside streams of water on a level path where they will not stumble. (Jeremiah 31:9)

At the end of the day:

_____
_____
_____
_____
_____
_____
_____
_____
_____
_____

FEBRUARY 6

YOU CAN GET THROUGH THIS

Everything that you are going through is setting you up for your blessings that God has for your life. Fact is life hurts and it is painful but it is worth living for.

Today, as hard as you hurt and as bad as it seems; know that God has already called you victorious. You are going to get through this.... the enemy can't win. You are fighting through these bad days to earn the best days of your life.

Remember, tough times and trouble don't last always, but tough people do! You weren't built to break!

These hard times will lead to the greatest moments of your life. Keep the Faith. It will all be worth it in the end.

My grace is sufficient for you, for my power is made perfect in weakness. (2 Corinthians 12:9)

Stay Prayed Up & Encouraged ~ I'm Praying for YOU

At the end of the day:

_____
_____
_____
_____
_____
_____
_____
_____
_____

FEBRUARY 7

YOU ARE

Today, don't let what someone said to you define you. You are not what they say, but what God says!

A lot of times someone will tell you what they think you are. When in reality they have no idea that YOU are a child of the most High God. "Do not touch my anointed ones, and do my prophets no harm." (1 Chronicles 16:22)

You are Beautiful! (Song of Solomon 4:7)

You are Strong! (Peter 5:10)

You are Important! (1 Peter 2:9)

You are Forgiven! (2 Chronicles 7:14)

You are Protected! (Psalm 121:7)

You are Empowered! (Acts 1:8)

You are Loved! (Romans 5:8)

And most of all, God says that YOU are Mine! (Isaiah 43:1)

So, hold your head back up. YOU are God's child!

I have written to you who are God's children because you know the Father. I have written to you who are mature in the faith because you know Christ, who existed from the beginning. I have written to you who are young in the faith because you are strong. God's word lives in your heart and you have won your battle with the evil one. (1 John 2:14)

At the end of the day:

_____

_____

_____

FEBRUARY 8

YOU ARE VICTORIOUS

When life throws us hard blows in the natural it can look like things aren't going to work out, but we know that Romans 8:28 says, "all things work for the good of those who love Him, who have been called according to His purpose."

Today, know that you are God's child and you are victorious! Life might have thrown you some blows, but you are walking in God's favor and honoring Him with your life knowing that nothing can defeat you. That temporary setback just set you up for your glorious comeback!

Know, in all these things we are more than conquerors through him who loved us." (Romans 8:37)

At the end of the day:

_____
_____
_____
_____
_____
_____
_____
_____
_____
_____
_____

FEBRUARY 9

YOU ARE IMPORTANT TO GOD

Even though it looks like the enemy is winning and you are being defeated, God is your Vindicator. You matter to God! He is keeping track of everything that is happening to you and every single person that is doing you wrong. He will make up for every single tear you have shed.

Today, know that God is restoring to you everything that the enemy is and has ever tried to steal and has stolen from you. He is healing you from every pain, hurt and scar from your life. He wants you to know that weeping will be of no more because joy is here to stay!

You keep track of all my sorrows. You have collected all my tears in your bottle. You have recorded each one in your book. (Psalm 56:8)

At the end of the day:

_____
_____
_____
_____
_____
_____
_____
_____
_____
_____

FEBRUARY 10

YOU ARE COVERED

Worry, fear and anxiety are not from God. And although the situation looks bad… know that through it all, God has you covered. (Psalm 91:3)

Today you need to know that even though you are walking through the valley of the shadow of death, God is still with you. (Psalm 23:4) For His Word tells us that He will never leave nor forsake you. (Deuteronomy 31:6)

Remember, you have to stop worrying…because when was the last time God failed you? When was the last time He was late? And when was the last time He left you alone? Well, let me help you…. NEVER!

YOU ARE COVERED

Stay Prayed Up & Encouraged

He will cover you with his feathers. He will shelter you with his wings. His faithful promises are your armor and protection. (Psalm 91:4)

At the end of the day:

_____
_____
_____
_____
_____
_____
_____
_____

FEBRUARY 11

YOU ARE BLESSED

I know that your plate is full and you are feeling overwhelmed with everyday circumstances. But God hasn't forgotten about you. You are still highly favored and blessed.

Today, don't focus on everything that is going on. Instead realize through it all that God is still carrying you.

You might be and feel stressed right now, but God says, That you are still blessed!

Stay Prayed Up & Encouraged

Blessed are the poor in spirit, for theirs is the kingdom of heaven. Blessed are those who mourn, for they shall be comforted. "Blessed are the meek, for they shall inherit the earth. Blessed are those who hunger and thirst for righteousness, for they shall be satisfied. Blessed are the merciful, for they shall receive mercy. (Matthew 5:3-7)

At the end of the day:

_____
_____
_____
_____
_____
_____
_____

FEBRUARY 12

YOU ARE ANOINTED

I know you think you need help from the attorney to get you out of the trouble that you're in. You think that the "hook up" from your friend is going to get you in the door for the job you want, and that colleague is going to help you get the account that you desperately need so bad. But God says that you don't need anyone but Him!!!

Today you need to know that everything you have been begging and pleading for others to help you with, God has already anointed you with it. He has fixed it and worked it out on your behalf. My dear friends you have been anointed by the Holy One and you have all the knowledge and power that you need to get it done. (1 John 2:20)

You WILL NOT beg and plead for anyone to help you, not another day. YOU are God's Child!

As for you, the anointing which you received from Him abides in you, and you have no need for anyone to teach you; but as His anointing teaches you about all things, and is true and is not a lie, and just as it has taught you, you abide in Him. (1 John 2:27)

At the end of the day:

_____
_____
_____
_____
_____
_____
_____

FEBRUARY 13

YOU ARE A SOLDIER

Do you know that you are a soldier in The Lord's Army? God will complete His plan and purpose for your life. Never doubt and give up on God who is going to preserve and protect you from all harm.

Today, stand firm on the promises that God has said about your life. Have faith and believe; believe that He will give you the desires of your heart. But you need to use your spiritual weapons every day as a soldier. Pray without ceasing, read your Bible daily, and be obedient to His Word. Nothing is too hard for God! He loves us with an everlasting love.

Our soul waits for the LORD; He is our help and our shield. For our heart is glad in Him, because we trust in His holy name. Let your steadfast love, O LORD, be upon us, even as we hope in you. (Psalms 33:20-22)

At the end of the day:

_____
_____
_____
_____
_____
_____
_____
_____

FEBRUARY 14

YOU ALWAYS WIN

The enemy is something else! He tries to come at you from the North, South, East and West. That's why it is imperative that you stay in God's Word.

Today, tell the devil, "All I do is win." He thinks he is getting the best of you. But what he doesn't know is what he means for evil God means for your good! (Genesis 50:20)

Remember, you don't have to wait till the storm, trial or battle is over; you can go ahead and shout right now. Let God pour you out a blessing so great you won't have enough room to receive it! (Malachi 3:10)

Now get your praise on because God says YOU win!

Stay Prayed Up & Encouraged ~

But thanks be to God, who gives us the victory through our Lord Jesus Christ. (1 Corinthians 15:57)

At the end of the day:

_____
_____
_____
_____
_____
_____
_____
_____
_____

FEBRUARY 15

YOU ALREADY WON

If you are enduring a storm, trial or a test, best believe that God is at work in your life. Don't be afraid of thousands of enemies who surround you on every side. (Psalm 3:6) They may fall at your side and thousands at your right hand, but they will not touch you. (Psalm 91:7)

Today give thanks to God who has given us victory through our Lord Jesus Christ. (1 Corinthians 15:57) It is The Lord, your God who goes with you to fight your enemies and to give you the victory.

Remember, you may not be able to see it now, but God has already called this fight and you are the winner! (Deuteronomy 20:4)

For every child of God defeats this evil world, and we achieve this victory through our faith. And who can win this battle against the world? Only those who believe that Jesus is the Son of God. (1 John 5:4-5)

At the end of the day:

_____
_____
_____
_____
_____
_____
_____
_____
_____

FEBRUARY 16

YOU ALMOST

When the raging storms came into your life you almost gave up, but you knew God was still on The Throne. (Psalm 47:8) You almost let depression, anxiety and worry take over your life, but you knew where your help was coming from. (Psalm 121:2) You almost took your own life, but you refused to be a victim but a Victor. (Revelation 2:10) When people look at you now they know that you are a survivor and God has been on your side. (Psalm 118:6)

Give thanks this day because God has kept you. You almost...BUT you didn't... let go of His hand. (Isaiah 41:13)

Keeping you lifted in prayer,

At the end of the day:

FEBRUARY 17

YES....IT HAPPENED

Things might not have gone the way you planned. You've been sitting around telling yourself, "God I wasn't supposed to be here or why is this happening?"

Today it's time to recognize as hard and ugly as it looks and feels... IT happened. You need now to press toward the call of the prize. (Philippians 3:14) It's not the time to keep looking back and talking about coulda, shoulda and woulda's. But it is time to press forward!

Remember, your destiny is not determined by the number of times you fall. But it is determined by the number of times you get back up and rise again.

Forget the former things; do not dwell on the past. See, I am doing a new thing. Now it springs up; do you not perceive it? I am making a way in the wilderness and streams in the wasteland. (Isaiah 43:18-19)

At the end of the day:

FEBRUARY 18

WISHY WASHY

People can be wishy washy. They will say that they are going to do this or that, make commitments and won't do it or have a covenant and then break it. But God is consistent and if He said it, He will surely do it.

Today know that God is not like man that he should lie, He will not keep changing His mind. If He has spoken it He will fulfill it. (Numbers 23:19)

Remember, what God has started in your life, He will finish.

So, God has given both His promise and His oath. These two things are unchangeable because it is impossible for God to lie. Therefore, we who have fled to Him for refuge can have great confidence as we hold to the hope that lies before us. (Hebrews 6:18)

At the end of the day:

_____
_____
_____
_____
_____
_____
_____
_____
_____

FEBRUARY 19

WHY YOU KEEP PICKING ON ME?

Do you ever wonder why the enemy won't leave you alone? I mean you keep on working for The Lord and doing what is right, but every time you turn around Satan is knocking at your door. Well, when you are truly dedicated and living for Christ, you will be targeted and picked on.

Today, know that you may have gotten picked on; but that's because Satan knows that you are anointed and God is about to open up the windows of Heaven just for you. But little does he know God is fighting the battle for you.

Remember, no need to fret or get discouraged. You have the best secret weapon on the earth. GOD!

You did not choose me, but I chose you and appointed you that you should go and bear fruit and that your fruit should abide, so that whatever you ask the Father in my name, He may give it to you. (John 15:16

At the end of the day:

_____
_____
_____
_____
_____
_____
_____
_____

FEBRUARY 20

Why You Are Trying to Figure It Out? When He is Already Working It Out

It's easy to get so focused on what you are going through that you forget that all things work together for the good of them that love The Lord. (Romans 8:28)

Today, just leave all your problems alone and stop trying to figure it out. God has you in the palm of His hands. (Isaiah 49:16) He is The Lord and you don't need to fear because He is helping you. (Isaiah 41:13)

Remember, The Lord is your strength, rock, fortress, deliverer and savior. In Him, you will find protection and refuge. Keep calling out to Him and you will be saved from your enemies and trials.

For God is working in you, giving you the desire and the power to do what pleases Him. (Philippians 2:13)

At the end of the day:

_____
_____
_____
_____
_____
_____
_____
_____
_____
_____

FEBRUARY 21

WHO DID YOU TELL?

Many people sit around and will gossip about what someone did or didn't do, will talk about a reality tv show, will rave about a celebrity and what they had on but you rarely hear people talking about God's goodness. Then they wonder why they are in the position that they're in.

Today, know that you must talk daily about God's goodness if you want to see His favor and protection. Stop talking about what's wrong in your life and start talking about how wonderful and magnificent God is.

The bigger you talk about God, the smaller your problem and situation gets.

Magnify and Glorify His Name!

Let the one who boasts, boast in the Lord. (2 Corinthians 10:17)

At the end of the day:

FEBRUARY 22

WHO ARE YOU SEEKING

God rewards those who earnestly seek after Him. I know life can be hard. If you want a man or woman what do you usually do? You chase after them. You want a new pair of shoes...so, you chase after them... looking high and low. You want a new car...a particular color...what do you do? Search high and low on the internet until you find it. But are you seeking after the Father?

Today, if you truly want God to bless you, you will follow and obey His commands. If you are faithful to Him, He will reward you like nothing you have ever seen before. But you have to be a God chaser! Quit chasing after stuff and make up your mind today that you will diligently seek after Him.

But seek first the kingdom of God and his righteousness, and all these things will be added to you. (Matthew 6:33)

At the end of the day:

FEBRUARY 23

WHEN YOU BELIEVE, GOD WORKS

Nothing is impossible with God. (Luke 1:37) But you must believe. When you believe that God is one; you are going to prosper. Even the demons believe and they start to shake in their boots! (James 2:19)

Today know that without faith it is impossible to please God for whoever would draws near to Him must believe that He exists and that He rewards those who seek Him. (Hebrews 11:6)

Remember, whatever you ask in prayer, you will receive, if you have faith! (Matthew 21:22)

So that your faith might not rest in the wisdom of men but in the power of God. (1 Corinthians 2:5)

At the end of the day:

___
___
___
___
___
___
___
___
___
___
___

FEBRUARY 24

WHEN IT DOESN'T MAKE SENSE

Life can be hard, but it is worth living for. Sometimes when you have been knocked down and you can't understand why things are happening in your life; that is when you have to lean on The Lord the most.

Today don't be surprised at the fiery trials you are going through, as if something strange were happening to you. Instead, be glad and get your "happy" on. For these trials make you partners with Christ in His suffering, so that you will have the wonderful joy of seeing His glory when it is revealed. (1 Peter 4:12-13)

Remember, it might not make sense now, but one day you will understand why you had to go through this.

These trials will show that your faith is genuine. It is being tested as fire tests and purifies gold, though your faith is far more precious than mere gold. So, when your faith remains strong through many trials, it will bring you much praise and glory and honor on the day when Jesus Christ is revealed to the whole world. (1 Peter 1:7)

At the end of the day:

_____
_____
_____
_____
_____
_____
_____

FEBRUARY 25

WHEN GOD IS IN IT

Life might have thrown you some curve balls and you might feel overwhelmed and defeated. But things aren't always as they appear!

Today you need to know that God says, there is no pit deep enough that He can't pull you up out of.

There is no fire so hot that he cannot shield you from....and there is definitely not a storm you're in that He can't protect and cover you from.

Remember, God's plan is the best plan...and sometimes it's difficult, hurtful and even painful. But don't forget, when He's silent that is when He is doing His best work for YOU!!!

That is why, for Christ's sake, I delight in weaknesses, in insults, in hardships, in persecutions, in difficulties. For when I am weak, then I am strong. (2 Corinthians 12:10)

At the end of the day:

_____
_____
_____
_____
_____
_____
_____
_____

FEBRUARY 26

WHATCHA GONNA DO?

Are you going to sit there and just lay out because you feel lost and alone? Or are you going to continue to stay in bed day after day and cry & cry? Either way they are both tricks and lies from the enemy to keep you defeated.

Today you must cease and resist any victimized behavior. YOU WILL NOT DIE!!!! Fact is God is looking at you and wants to see how you are going to handle this turmoil.

So, this isn't the time nor place to sit up in a balled-up knot and position yourself to die. But it is the time to count it all joy for the hell you are enduring. (James 1:2)

Remember, this isn't the time to shrink.... but it is the time to step into your greatness and that's what you're gonna do!

At the end of the day:

FEBRUARY 27

WHAT YOU SAY?

The words you speak matter. It's imperative that you watch what you say because the tongue is powerful and it can bring death or life. (Proverbs 18:21)

Today, know that if you keep talking and speaking as if you can't, you won't, and you will never have; you're speaking it into existence. You are more than a conqueror! You can do all things through Him who gives you strength. (Philippians 4:13)

Remember, Your words have the power to affect your joy, your prayers and your future." - Joyce Meyers

Let no corrupting talk come out of your mouths, but only such as is good for building up, as fits the occasion, that it may give grace to those who hear. (Ephesians 4:29)

At the end of the day:

_____
_____
_____
_____
_____
_____
_____
_____
_____
_____
_____

FEBRUARY 28

WHAT IT CAUSED

In this life, you will be up and then you will be down. Trials and tribulations, you can't run from. But in the end…. you will understand what it has caused you.

Today know that through all the tears, pain and sorrow — God still had a plan for you. It might have looked like the enemy was winning and you were counted out. But thank God, we walk by Faith and not by sight! (2 Corinthians 5:7)

Remember, if you had to take back all the hurt that the enemy caused…you would also have to return the strength that you gained in the process!

Now look at what it caused!

Stay Prayed Up & Encouraged ~Do not be grieved, for the joy of the LORD is your strength. (Nehemiah 8:10)

At the end of the day:
_____
_____
_____
_____
_____
_____
_____
_____
_____

MARCH 1

YOU CAN'T HIDE

God sees and hears everything. There is nothing that is going on that you can't escape and get away from Him from. He knows the things that you don't even want Him to know. The good, the bad, the ugly and the wicked. (Proverbs 15:3)

Today you have to know that you can't hide and run from The Lord. His eyes are on your ways and there is nothing that you have done that can be concealed from Him. (Jeremiah 16:17)

Remember, there are no secrets that time does not reveal. (Jean Racine)

Nothing in all creation is hidden from God. Everything is naked and exposed before his eyes, and he is the one to whom we are accountable. (Hebrews 4:13)

At the end of the day:

_____
_____
_____
_____
_____
_____
_____
_____
_____
_____

MARCH 2

YOU CAN'T BREAK NOW

That break up, the divorce and that crazy job that practically landed you to take every anxiety pill out there; still can't break you!

Today, I want you to tell the devil, "look at me now....and I'm still here." He thought he would catch you slipping and creep on in... but the devil is a lie. What he meant for evil, God meant for your good and all things work out for the good of those who love The Lord. (Genesis 50:20) (Romans 8:28)

Remember, it's at that very moment when you're about to give up, when your breakthrough will occur. So just keep holding on, because God is up to something.

Stay Prayed Up & Encouraged Up ~

Let us hold fast the confession of our hope without wavering, for He who promised is faithful. (Hebrews 10:23)

At the end of the day:

MARCH 3

YOU CAN'T BE SILENT

We all have a story. Whether good or bad, there is a testimony that you have that someone can benefit from. You never know who sits alone in the dark weeping about the storm they are in. You could be the very thing that can assist in picking them up. Please don't be silent.

Today share your testimony with someone so they can be lifted. God has done and will continue to do mighty things in your life. Let others know how He brought you through.

Remember, only God can turn a mess into a message, a test into a testimony, a trial into a triumph and a victim into a victory.

Jesus did not let him, but said, "Go home to your own people and tell them how much the Lord has done for you, and how He has had mercy on you. (Mark 5:19)

At the end of the day:

_____
_____
_____
_____
_____
_____
_____
_____
_____
_____

MARCH 4

WHAT DID YOU JUST SAY?

This week I too was speaking words that was bringing me down and that was causing my funk. To sum it up I was inviting the devil in. THAT IS A LIE!!! I REBUKE AND CAST HIM OUT! I know I am a work in progress and every day I have to put off the breastplate of righteousness and fight off the wicked realms of evil. I look at it like this, I have been in advertising for over 14 years and have seen the power of words affect buying decisions and so forth. With saying that, we set the tone over ourselves with the words we say. If I say I am in a funk, well then I will be in a funk. WHAT YOU SAY ABOUT YOURSELF HAS POWER! Our words can keep us from the promises that God has for us to come. As soon as you speak something good or bad, you have just given it life! So be careful of what you speak out loud!

You Say, "I Can't Figure It Out" BUT, God Says, "I Will Direct Your Steps."(Proverbs 3:5-6)

You Say, "It's Impossible" BUT, God Says, "All Things Are Possible." (Luke:18:27)

You Say, "I'm Not Able" BUT, God Says, "I'm Able." (II Corinthians 9:8)

You Say, "I Can't Do It" BUT, God Says, "You Can Do All Things." (Philippians 4:13)

You Say, "I Don't Have" BUT, God Says, "I Will Supply All Your Needs." (Philippians 4:19)

You Say, "I'm Afraid", BUT, God Says, "I Have Not Given You Fear." (II Timothy 1:7)

You Say, "I Feel Alone", BUT, God Says, "I Will Never Leave You"

(Hebrews 13:5)

You Say, "I'm Not Smart Enough", BUT, God Says, "I Will Give You Wisdom." (1 Corinthians 1:30)

So This Week You Will Say You Are A Child Of The High Most God and You Walk in Dominion, Favor & You're Highly Blessed.

At the end of the day:

_____
_____
_____
_____
_____
_____
_____
_____
_____
_____
_____
_____
_____
_____
_____
_____
_____
_____
_____
_____
_____

MARCH 5

WHAT ARE YOU LOOKING AT?

Every situation we will face, God already has an answer and solution for. He is the answer!

Today, don't focus on what is going on, why or how you are in the biggest storm of your life. But reevaluate who you are focusing on. Things in the natural can always cause us to think it's worse than it really is. But it's only because you have taken your eyes off of Jesus.

So, get your glasses, sun glasses or contact lenses on and get focused in on the One, THE ONLY ONE, who is going to get you out of your storm.

If you want the victory, keep your eyes on Him...He won't let you down.

Fixing our eyes on Jesus, the author and perfecter of faith, who for the joy set before Him endured the cross, despising the shame, and has sat down at the right hand of the throne of God. (Hebrews 12:2)

At the end of the day:

MARCH 6

WATCH WHAT I CAN DO

God is a God who works wonders. He has revealed His might among nations. (Psalm 77:14) Even the demons believe this and they tremble in terror. (James 2:19) There is nothing too hard for The Lord to do for you. (Jeremiah 32:27) God wants us to trust Him and have that mustard seed type of Faith. He wants you to believe in your heart that if you tell a mountain to move from here to there that it will move and nothing will be impossible for you. (Matthew 17:20)

Today you need to stop doubting and focusing on what it looks like. Cry out to God and tell Him that you have Faith as small as a mustard seed and you are turning everything over to Him... and watch what He will do in your life. (Matthew 21:21) You must believe and fully trust God to see you through your storm, and no one else. God is the only one that is going to restore and resurrect what has been taken from you. (Joel 2:25-26)

So, STOP letting your Faith rest on how a man or woman can get you out of this, but on the POWER of God! (1 Corinthians 2:5)

Know that a person is not justified by the works of the law, but by faith in Jesus Christ. So, we, too, have put our faith in Christ Jesus that we may be justified by faith in Christ and not by the works of the law, because by the works of the law no one will be justified. (Galatians 2:16)

At the end of the day:

_____
_____
_____
_____

MARCH 7

WALK VICTORIOUSLY

It's important in this life to have the attitude of knowing who you are and whose you are. In all these things, we are more than conquerors through Him who loved us. (Romans 8:37)

Today, walk like you know it. No matter what you face or the circumstances that you are enduring. Take up the shield of faith so you can extinguish all the flaming darts of the evil one. (Ephesians 6:16)

Remember, the God of peace will soon crush Satan under your feet; and the grace of our Lord Jesus Christ will be with you. (Romans 16:20)

For the Lord, your God is He who goes with you to fight for you against your enemies, to give you the victory. (Deuteronomy 20:4)

At the end of the day:

MARCH 8

WALK LIKE YOU ALREADY KNOW

When you are going through something and the enemy is telling you one thing, it is easy to get down and discouraged. But you must recognize that the devil's job is to kill and destroy! (John 10:10) He is the father of lies, (John 8:44) and he wants to deceive you. (Revelation 20:10)

Today walk like you know who you are and more importantly who you belong too! You are a child of the highest God. (Galatians 3:26) You might have the enemy attacking by the thousands right now and that has you feeling overwhelmed, but you're not defeated. Sure, they are coming, but God won't let them touch you. (Psalm 91:7)

Remember, your boots are made for walking so that is what you need to do. Walk like you know who you belong to!!!

Even though I walk through the darkest valley, I will fear no evil, for you are with me; your rod and your staff, they comfort me. (Psalm 23:4)

At the end of the day:

_____
_____
_____
_____
_____
_____
_____
_____

MARCH 9

WALK BY FAITH

If you really want to please God, you are going to have to activate your Faith. I know you are praying and needing God to move and work in your life, but can you say that you are truly walking by Faith?

Today, let's get God's angels to move on your behalf by trusting Him and believing that He will do what He said He will do. If we really want God to change our circumstances He needs to see that we have Faith, and without Faith it is impossible to please God. (Hebrews 11:6)

So, walk by Faith and not by sight and show God what you are really made of! (2 Corinthians 5:7)

Now faith is confidence in what we hope for and assurance about what we do not see. (Hebrews 11:1)

At the end of the day:

MARCH 10

WAKE UP

It truly saddens me to see kids going down the wrong path, husbands disrespecting their wives, wives cheating on their husbands and siblings not speaking to one another. I can go on and on but you get the picture. It comes a time where you got to say to self, "this isn't what I want". There are consequences to all of our actions in this world. We can't keep living and thinking that we are "good", because you will reap what you sow.

Do not be deceived: God is not mocked, for whatever one sows, that will he also reap. (Galatians 6:7)

Whether you are an employer and you are a very hateful boss you will get "your day". Whether you are an employee and you are skimming from your employer you will get "your day". I don't care who you are, the seeds you sow - if they are foul - will come back foul on you. You must remember: God is close to the brokenhearted. He hears their cries!

The Lord is near to the brokenhearted and saves the crushed in spirit. (Psalm 34:18)

Unfortunately, so many people are afraid to admit when they are wrong or out of order. Instead they move to a position of pride. Once there, it's easier to lie, make excuses and ignore personal issues, rather than face them in humility. In God's plan, pride becomes an obstacle that halts His mercy. You must remove pride so you can receive God's full blessings!

Let the wicked forsake his way, and the unrighteous man his thoughts; and let him return to the LORD, and He will have compassion on him; and to our God, for He will abundantly pardon. (Isaiah 55:7)

At the end of the day:

MARCH 11

WAITING TIME... ISN'T WASTED TIME

We tend to get impatient when we feel like things we have prayed for aren't going our way or coming to pass. But we have to put our trust in The Lord and know that God hasn't left nor forgotten about us. What He is doing is developing, building and polishing you so that when the right time comes you will be able to Soar Powerful like an Eagle that God has molded and called you to be!

Just hold on...Help is on the way

But they who wait for the Lord shall renew their strength; they shall mount up with wings like eagles; they shall run and not be weary; they shall walk and not faint. (Isaiah 40:31)

At the end of the day:

_____
_____
_____
_____
_____
_____
_____
_____
_____
_____
_____
_____
_____

MARCH 12

WAIT A MINUTE

It's easy to become discouraged when you have prayed and cried while standing for God to move mountains through the difficulties you are facing in your life. I know you may feel tired and weary from the spiritual battle you're in right now. But the good news is, those who wait on The Lord shall renew their strength.

Today, get your pep back in your step and wait gracefully and patiently while God restores any and everything that has been wrongfully taken from you. The Victory is Yours!

But they that wait upon the LORD shall renew their strength; they shall mount up with wings as eagles; they shall run, and not be weary; and they shall walk, and not faint. (Isaiah 40:31)

At the end of the day:

_____
_____
_____
_____
_____
_____
_____
_____
_____
_____

MARCH 13

VICTORY IS MINE

It often feels a lot of times that things are done unfairly and you get the wrong end of the stick. Always know that God promises that He will never leave nor forsake you.

Stop speaking about what is not working out and what is going wrong in your lives and start talking about what you know and who your God is. Declare and Decree right now that you already got the Victory and the devil is a lie!

And we know that in all things God works for the good of those who love him, who have been called according to his purpose. (Romans 8:28)

At the end of the day:

_____
_____
_____
_____
_____
_____
_____
_____
_____
_____
_____
_____
_____

MARCH 14

TURN YOUR WORRY INTO WORSHIP

It's easy to get down, cry, vent, lie in bed all day or just get so caught up in what you are going through that you feel so overwhelmed that you don't know what to do. Reality is that there is something you can do, and that is get your praise on and get a Word from The Lord.

Casting all your anxieties on Him, because He cares f or you. (1 Peter 5:7)

Stop giving the enemy your time and energy by worrying over things that God is already in control over. God wants us to be free from worry. In The Bible, it says in Luke 12, "God will provide." So, I want to encourage all of you today that I don't care WHAT IT IS!!!!! And trust me WE ALL have a "WHAT" Get your praise on today and get in your word!

God is getting ready to deliver us from worry by focusing our attention on His faithfulness and His Kingdom!!! Put all your trust in Him and seek Him first always! When you do, it's His promise to you that you will be free from worry.

Sow seeds from resources you have been given, and it's His promise to you that you will Reap…and your burden will be lifted!

At the end of the day:

_____
_____
_____
_____
_____

MARCH 15

TURN THE PAGE

Sometimes it can be hard to walk away from a relationship, divorce, friendship or even a job. If "they" have left and walked away from you...there is no need in begging, using trickery schemes trying to get them back, or filing law suits and sitting around moping. Let them go!

Today, know that in the end it just means that God never meant for them to be a part of your destiny. The part of their story is over for them. Now Turn Your Page to New Beginnings!

Remember not the former things, nor consider the things of old. Behold, I am doing a new thing; now it springs forth, do you not perceive it? I will make a way in the wilderness and rivers in the desert. (Isaiah 43:18-19)

At the end of the day:

_____
_____
_____
_____
_____
_____
_____
_____
_____
_____
_____
_____

MARCH 16

TRUST THE LORD

See, God has come to save me. I will trust in him and not be afraid. The LORD God is my strength and my song; he has given me victory. (Isaiah 12:2)

How many of you put your money in the bank or credit union?

    How many of you buy items online?

    How many of you drive vehicles every day?

    How many of you eat at restaurants?

I'm sure you had to say yes to at least one or all of them. If you trust your money with a banker, trust eBay/PayPal, and cars on the streets, or even cooks not to poison your food...why can't you trust our Heavenly Father?

I've come to learn that God wants His people to prosper in all that they set their hearts on. You have to keep enduring, even when the enemy is making it hard for you. (That's how you know God is getting ready to bless you.

The Lord is our refuge and strength, no matter what is knocking at our door! You are a child of the Most High God.... YOU are covered by the blood of Jesus Christ!! There is no need to fear, worry or be dismayed.... God's got this!

At the end of the day:

_____

_____

_____

_____

MARCH 17

TRUST HIS PROCESS

It can be frustrating when we don't understand things and it doesn't make sense to us at all. But you must know that God does see the big picture. Just when you think that door that got slammed in your face broke you, God was really behind the door saving you from harm.

Today, be safe and secure and know that just because you don't understand what God is always doing... trust and know that He sees the big picture. Just because you are ready...God hasn't placed the right person in your life yet! So be patient and trust His process.

And those who know your name put their trust in you, for you, O Lord, have not forsaken those who seek you. Psalm 9:10

At the end of the day:

_____
_____
_____
_____
_____
_____
_____
_____
_____
_____

MARCH 18

TROUBLE, DRAMA, & TRAUMA

So many people are going through right now, that if you had to sum it up it, equals to "TDT" Trouble, Drama and Trauma. Although some of you are running to Iyanla to fix your life; may I suggest you need to be running to The Lord.

Today you must know that the devil is a lie!!!! God is not a God of confusion and trouble can't last always!!! (1 Corinthians 14:33) What feels like it is killing you is really stretching and growing you. If you never had been stretched or crushed, you never would know such glory & favor from The Lord.

Remember, your great reward is coming! And you will be blessed for the sufferings you've had to endure. But my dear brothers & sisters, YOU have to hold on and continue to stand.....it's necessary!!!!(James 1:2), (Matthew 5:10-12) & (1 Corinthians 15:1)

Be on guard. Stand firm in the faith. Be courageous. Be strong. (1 Corinthians 16:13)

At the end of the day:

_____
_____
_____
_____
_____
_____
_____
_____

MARCH 19

TROUBLE DON'T LAST ALWAYS

You might be feeling that no one could possibly understand what you are going through. They haven't felt the type of pain, rejection and hurt that you are facing today. (So, you think) But God says, "I am with you and will watch over you, wherever you go. Even when you fall I will pick you back up. I will not leave you until I have done what I have promised you." (Genesis 28:15)

Today wipe the tears from your eyes, pick your head up and put a smile on that beautiful face. God has plans to prosper you, to give you a future and a hope. (Jeremiah 29:11) He will keep His promise!

Remember, don't look at the troubles you can see now; but fix your eyes on things that cannot be seen. For the things you see now will soon be gone, but the things you cannot see will last forever. (2 Corinthians 4:18)

Yet what we suffer now is nothing compared to the glory He will reveal to us later. (Romans 8:18)

At the end of the day:

_____
_____
_____
_____
_____
_____
_____
_____

MARCH 20

TRAGEDY TO TRIUMPH

Everything happens for a reason. That is a saying that in one way or another we all have heard. Fact is you may not understand it today, but one day you will. I know that you are hurting. I know that you can't even pray for yourself or cry any more tears, but fact is you are on your way out of the storm. It can't rain forever and every break eventually heals.

Today and moving forward don't focus on your tragedy but focus on the fact that because He loves you so much that He has already given you the victory. (Romans 8:37)

Remember, your testimony is going to be a blessing to another; and you can't have the testimony without having the test! So, keep your head up.... it's almost over!

But thanks be to God, who in Christ always leads us in triumphal procession, and through us spreads the fragrance of the knowledge of Him everywhere. (2 Corinthians 2:14)

At the end of the day:

_____
_____
_____
_____
_____
_____
_____

MARCH 21

TRADE IT

God doesn't want you holding on to the pain, hurt and brokenness from the past. He needs to see the pain traded for comfort. The hurt traded for healing and the brokenness traded for completeness and wholeness.

Today know that it's time for you to see beauty for the ashes you've endured. Your victory is NOW and The Lord takes great delight on His children and gives them the crown of victory. (Psalm 149:4)

Remember, a caterpillar once thought it's world was completely over. Then it turned into a beautiful butterfly!

HOLD ON!!!

He will give a crown of beauty for ashes, a joyous blessing instead of mourning, festive praise instead of despair. In their righteousness, they will be like great oaks that the LORD has planted for his own glory. (Isaiah 61:3)

At the end of the day:

_____
_____
_____
_____
_____
_____
_____
_____
_____

MARCH 22

TOUCH NOT MY ANOINTED

For many of you that feel like you just can't take one more blow from the enemy, because that last hit could be the one that will take you out. You need to know that God has made it very clear in Chronicles16:22 "Do not touch my anointed ones and do my prophets no harm." There will be a price to pay once you mess with a child of God. Continue to let them stir up strife and do evil. They can even mock you, but the wrath of the Lord will come upon them and He will punish those that are coming for you. (2 Chronicles 36:16)

Today hold your head up and know that you are God's child. He will take revenge and will pay back for the wrong that has occurred; and in due time your enemies' feet will slip and their day of disaster will come. (Deuteronomy 32:35) It is the Lord that will judge between you and them. It will be The Lord that will handle them, but your hand should never touch them. (1 Samuel 24:12)

So, stop trying to take revenge, but leave room for God's wrath and anger, because it is written, It is mine to avenge; and I will repay says The Lord. (Romans 12:19)

He is the God who pays back those who harm me; he brings down the nations under me (2 Samuel 22:48)

At the end of the day:

_____
_____
_____
_____
_____

MARCH 23

TOO MANY TIMES

Too many times you have failed, felt broken and counted out.... But God! Fact is God is greater in you than he that is in the world. (1 John 4:4)

Today it doesn't matter how many times you did this and that. God still says, greater is YOU!!!

Remember, to succeed you must first improve, to improve you must practice, to practice you must first learn, to learn you must first fail. "Wesley Woo"

You, dear children, are from God and have overcome them, because the one who is in you is greater than the one who is in the world. (1 John 4:4)

At the end of the day:

MARCH 24

THROUGH IT ALL YOU'RE STILL STANDING

Whether it is a divorce, job loss, sickness, the end of a relationship or a death of a loved one; God is still seeing you through. Sometimes the unexpected can make you feel broken or hopeless. However, The Lord is with you and there is no need to feel alone or afraid. He is with you in this battle, and He won't let you fall; it is through Him you are becoming stronger! (Joshua 1:9)

Today don't focus on the losses but focus on where God is getting ready to take you. He is an awesome and magnificent God. Although you have cried and shed some tears, He is here to wipe all of them away. He wants to take away all your pain, mourning, sorrow and heartache. (Revelation 21:4)

Remember, when you have prayed and cried. And cried and prayed. Just stand!

For I know the plans I have for you, declares the LORD, plans to prosper you and not to harm you, plans to give you hope and a future. (Jeremiah 29:11)

At the end of the day:

_____
_____
_____
_____
_____
_____
_____

MARCH 25

DEFENDING A LIE

A lie can hurt to the core. Especially if you have no way of defending and proving that you're telling the truth. So, what do you do? Remain still and let the Lord fight on your behalf. (Exodus) 14:14 YES, it's easier said than done. However, truthful lips endure forever, but a lying tongue and lies are soon exposed (Proverbs 12:19)

Remember, a truth can walk naked, but a lie always needs to be dressed- (Khalil Gibran)

And you will know the truth, and the truth will set you free (John 8:32)

At the end of the day:

MARCH 26

THIS IS YOUR SEASON

There is something inside of you that you know that you are supposed to be doing, but for whatever reason, you keep putting it off. Today is the day that you act upon it. Your destiny stands before you. God has something amazing in your future, but you must step out on faith and walk in the blessings that God has just for YOU!!!

To everything there is a season, and a time to every purpose under the heaven (Ecclesiastes 3:1)

At the end of the day:

MARCH 27

THIS IS MY PROMISE TO YOU

How many of you know the story of Sarah from the Bible? God gave Sarah a promise that she would have a baby but she was way beyond childbearing years; and she found that very hard to believe and that the promise God said would never come to pass. Sarah was in doubt and tried to take matters in her own hands but God told her "I SAID YOU WILL HAVE A BABY." And that's exactly what happened.

Today, don't be like Sarah was at first. Don't sit there in doubt and talk yourself down and out of what God said about your life. You have to look past your circumstances and look to God! Be faithful and obedient, and He will bring your promise to pass!

Fully convinced that God was able to do what he had promised. (Romans 4:21

At the end of the day:

___
___
___
___
___
___
___
___
___
___

MARCH 28

THIS IS JUST THE BEGINNING

God created you and He created YOU for greatness! He doesn't want you to settle or be okay with just a little. God has something much bigger, better and victorious for you.

Every day give Him all praise, glory and honor for your current blessings. Know that God never performs His greatest victories in the past but they are performed in the future.

Today, stay prayed up, encouraged and never give up!

Get ready to embrace the blessing God has in store for YOUR future!

No eye has seen, no ear has heard, and no mind has imagined what God has prepared for those who love him. (1 Corinthians 2:9)

At the end of the day:

_____
_____
_____
_____
_____
_____
_____
_____
_____
_____
_____
_____

MARCH 29

THIS IS IT

You have been going through the storm lately and some days you feel as if a hurricane has come through and ripped your world upside down. But the Tsunami and Hurricane Katrina is over right now. This is it!!!

Today have the attitude and mindset that, THIS IS IT! This is it that you will continue to let the devil steal your joy. He might have tried to come at you every way, shape and form; but this is it. You are going to take control of your life and start over.

Remember, if you are waiting for a sign, THIS IS IT!

The Lord has done it this very day; let us rejoice today and be glad. (Psalm 118:24)

At the end of the day:

_____
_____
_____
_____
_____
_____
_____
_____
_____
_____
_____
_____

MARCH 30

THIS & THAT-THAT & THIS

There will always be a time in life that you feel you have been given an unlucky break. Times that you just want to throw in the towel and say, "God that's it...I'm done." And then there will be the times that you feel like you have no one to support you; because everyone you thought would be there, turned their backs on you. BUT ...There will NEVER be a time where God isn't there!

Today whatever you are dealing with in the natural, God is right by your side through it all. When you are in the courtroom, He's right there! In the doctor's office, He's right there! Even driving down the highway... He's still right there covering YOU!

Remember, there will always be this and that....and that and this. But none of it will ever cause God to leave YOU!!!!

When you go through deep waters, I will be with you. When you go through rivers of difficulty, you will not drown. When you walk through the fire of oppression, you will not be burned up; the flames will not consume you. For I am the LORD, your God, the Holy One of Israel, your Savior. (Isaiah 43:2-3)

At the end of the day:

_____
_____
_____
_____
_____
_____
_____

MARCH 31

THINK LIKE AND ACT LIKE A WINNER

Power and death are in the power of the tongue. (Proverbs 18:22) What you say about yourself and what comes out of your mouth is crucial. It's time to act like and start being who God says you are.

Today is the day that you hold your head back up and declare and decree yourself as victorious, a winner and a mighty warrior with the Lord. (Judges 6:12) Never forget that God is on your side...and He will be with you and strike down those that try to come against you. (Judges 6:16)

Remember, if you don't see yourself as a winner, then you cannot perform as a winner. (Zig Ziglar)

For we are his workmanship, created in Christ Jesus for good works, which God prepared beforehand, that we should walk in them. (Ephesians 2:10)

At the end of the day:

_____
_____
_____
_____
_____
_____
_____
_____
_____

APRIL 1

THEY SAID NO, GOD SAYS YES

Folks' response to you can be anything.

1.) No, I don't need you.
2.) No, we are not hiring right now.
3.) No, You are not qualified.
4.) No, I don't want you.
5.) No, not right now but I will think about it.

Today, thank God for the No's in your life. Because every time "they" said no, God said YES!

Remember, the devil thought he had you down; but God has you!

For all the promises of God find their Yes in Him. That is why it is through Him that we utter our Amen to God for His glory. (2 Corinthians 1:20)

At the end of the day:

_____
_____
_____
_____
_____
_____
_____
_____
_____
_____

APRIL 2

THEY GOTTA GO

Whatever you have been going through lately God needs you to know that demons and the enemies are no longer welcome in your space. And this is the day that they have to go!!!!!

Today the eviction notice is served and posted! No more stress, no more depression, and no more drama! It's time to call on the name of JESUS and tell the enemy.... he's gotta GO!

Remember, when you call on the name of Jesus...even demons will begin to shudder and tremble at the name!!! (James 2:19)

I have given you authority to trample on snakes and scorpions and to overcome all the power of the enemy; nothing will harm you. (Luke 10:19)

At the end of the day:

_____
_____
_____
_____
_____
_____
_____
_____
_____
_____
_____
_____

APRIL 3

THEY CAN'T STAND ME...
BUT THEY CAN'T STOP ME

The enemy comes strong like a fiery dart trying to kill and destroy. But you have to thank God for your haters and enemies, because as much as they can't stand you and they try to take you out.... they still can't stop YOU!!!!!

Today give God praise and glory for everything that the enemy has been trying to do. It's time for you to look that snaggle-tooth enemy straight in the face and tell them, "Don't you dare gloat over me because I have fallen for now. I might sit in darkness for the meantime, but I will rise again. For the Lord will be my light!" (Micah 7:8)

Remember, they can't stop what they can't catch.... And the Lord is keeping you from all evil!

May the LORD judge between you and me. And may the LORD avenge the wrongs you have done to me, but my hand will not touch you. (1 Samuel 24:12)

At the end of the day:

_____
_____
_____
_____
_____
_____
_____

APRIL 4

THEY BETTER WATCH IT

The enemy is so out of God's will that He has no clue who he's messing with. You've been crying and getting upset all in a tizzy. When in actuality it's your adversary that needs to watch it!

Today you don't have to hide and stress anymore. You belong to God! And the fact is you don't need to be scared…but your enemy does!

Remember, if you know the enemy and know yourself. Well then you don't have to fear the results of a hundred battles. (Sum Tzu)

Do not touch my anointed ones, and do My prophets no harm. (1 Chronicles 16:22)

At the end of the day:

APRIL 5

THERE IS A REASON FOR IT

You may not realize it now but your pain does have a purpose. The tears, the struggle and the heartache you've endured will be worth it in the end.

Today, be encouraged because there is a reward for your faithfulness.

Remember, the struggle is real; but God only puts us through as much as He knows we can handle.

So, if you are struggling, count it all joy because you have been chosen by God and He knows that you are strong and can deal with it!

I can do all things through Him who strengthens me. (Philippians 4:13)

At the end of the day:

_____
_____
_____
_____
_____
_____
_____
_____
_____
_____

APRIL 6

THE TRUTH HURTS

It is easy to look at someone that seems to "have it all" the house, the cars, even the looks, but looks can be deceiving. Especially when you are having to put up a front that your life is all peachy perfect, faking like you are happily married when you are actually living in hell in your marriage or perpetuating that your 9 to 5 is bigger than what you make it seem. The biggest fraud that comes to mind that you all witness probably every day, without even knowing it, is being perpetuated via Face Book, Twitter, Instagram and other Social Media websites; when people make others think they have or are something that their actually not.

Having to call someone out about their "truth" can be hard, especially when they are not in a position to hear it. Some people might cuss and blow up on you, others might close and roll their eyes like you aren't saying anything at all, they might even try to mock you, or go as far as hiding from the truth by avoiding you and making excuses, or they might be quick to want to call out any flaws they think you have, in order to switch it around. There are some crazy people that get so mad at hearing the truth that they want to fight you for calling them out.

John 3:19-20 reads, "And this is the condemnation, that the light has come into the world, and men loved darkness rather than light, because their deeds were evil. For everyone practicing evil hates the light and does not come to the light, lest his deeds should be exposed." That said it all, family and friends!!!! Even though Light has come into the world, fact is some people love darkness so much that they reject the Light just so they can keep their evil deeds hidden. Which is why when you are trying to tell someone about their "truth" they don't even want to consider it could possibly be true, and that their "truth" is their Light?

At the end of the day:

APRIL 7

THE SUN & THE SON

It may seem very hard to see the "Son" in all the rain that you are standing in. But if you will just continue to stand strong, bow your head and say a prayer; you will weather this thunderstorm.

Remember, yes it might be pouring down now, but the sun will shine again!

Then the righteous will shine like the sun in the kingdom of their Father. Whoever has ears, let them hear. (Matthew 13:43)

At the end of the day:

_____
_____
_____
_____
_____
_____
_____
_____
_____
_____
_____
_____
_____
_____
_____
_____
_____

APRIL 8

THE STRUGGLE IS REAL

I hear a lot of the young kids now talking about the struggle is real. What I really want to tell them is, "What possibly in the world do you know about the struggle?" If you can recite scriptures when you are getting up in the morning and before you go to bed at night just so you won't lose your mind, well then you know about the struggle. For anyone that is in pain, agony or just hurting you know what the struggle really is.

Today, as you awake and get your day started, know that all the pain you are feeling has a purpose. God is stretching and molding you, and before He gives you the riches and glory to The Land you are going to have to go through some things. When it is all said and done you will be able to tell your friends, "I've had some good days and I have had some bad days, but when I think about all that God has done for me... my SOUL CRIES OUT!

So, keep your head up and stay in The Word. This too shall pass!

More than that, we rejoice in our sufferings, knowing that suffering produces endurance, and endurance produces character, and character produces hope, and hope does not put us to shame, because God's love has been poured into our hearts through the Holy Spirit who has been given to us. (Romans 5:3-5)

At the end of the day:

_____
_____
_____
_____

APRIL 9

THE STRENGTH TO DEAL WITH IT

Oftentimes we get bad news and the first thing that comes to mind is, "how am I going to get through this?" The reality is, God is with us throughout every step of our lives. Every storm, hurricane, disaster and even obstacle we face...He is there. He gives us the strength and grace to endure everything and anything in this life.

Today, know that God is your very present help in times of need. All you have to do is call out to Him and He will be right there.

There is Grace in the storms!

God is our refuge and strength, a very present help in trouble. (Psalm 46:1)

At the end of the day:

_____
_____
_____
_____
_____
_____
_____
_____
_____
_____

APRIL 10

THE STORM IS OVER

Blessed is the one who perseveres under trial because, having stood the test, that person will receive the crown of life that the Lord has promised to those who love him. (James 1:12)

Many of us are going through the storm right now. It seems our problems are overwhelming us and we think we are going under. In Psalms 125:1 it says, that those who put their trust in God are immovable like Mount Zion. God wants us to know that we may get tired and weary and you may get wet.... But YOU WILL MAKE IT! (That's HIS promise to YOU!)

NEWSFLASH We are not here on earth just to take up space.... God has a specific purpose and plan for our lives. Storms are simply temporary setbacks toward fulfilling that purpose. There is ABSOLUTELY NOTHING that can change God's ultimate purpose for our lives...unless we choose to disobey Him. The Bible teaches us that no outside person can change what God has ordained for our lives... NO ONE! Know today that God's purpose is greater than any problem you are ever going to experience. God has a plan beyond the storm that is in your life right now. Anchor yourself on the truth of God and pray.

God keeps His promises always without fail. The storms we are in cannot hide our faces from God...He is always with us. We may not see Him, but He sees us. Storms cannot change the purpose of God, nor can they destroy a child of God. God says, Never will I leave you; never will I forsake you. (Hebrews 13:5)

At the end of the day:

_____

_____

_____

APRIL 11

THE SITUATION

Often when you are in a situation all you can see is "the situation". The enemy can play so many tricks with you, making you feel like it won't get better at all. But that's a lie!!!

Today you have to stop looking at what it looks like because it's temporary. When you are going through something, it does hurt and it doesn't feel good at all. But if you would continue to hold onto God's unchanging hand and be immovable, you will see that you will win this race.

Remember, you may not be able to control every situation you get in.... but you can believe that God has the situation under control.

So, we fix our eyes not on what is seen, but on what is unseen, since what is seen is temporary, but what is unseen is eternal. (2 Corinthians 4:18)

At the end of the day:

_____
_____
_____
_____
_____
_____
_____
_____
_____
_____

APRIL 12

TOO STRONG TO LET THEM TEAR YOU DOWN

Fearfully and wonderfully made YOU ARE! From the moment that you were in your mother's womb GOD set you apart and made you magnificent. (Psalm 139 13-16) So, don't let what "they" say affect you.

Today, pick your beautiful head back up and put your shoulders back and walk like you know WHO you are and WHOSE you are. You are a child of the Most High God. (Psalm 82:6)

Truth is you have already overcome, because the one who's in you is greater than the one who's in the world. (1 John 4:4)

Remember, you are too strong to live hurt. You are too beautiful to let someone's ugly ways make you insecure with yourself. (Trent Shelton)

I praise you, for I am fearfully a wonderfully mad. Wonderful are your works, my soul knows it very well. (Psalm 139:14)

At the end of the day:

___
___
___
___
___
___
___
___

APRIL 13

THE ROAD TO VICTORY

You might have been driving down a dark and dreary road, but God has stepped in right on time. He has promised to never leave nor forsake you and what was looking like gloom and doom is now looking bright and sunny! (Deuteronomy 31:6)

Today, is the day that you get back on track. It's time to declare and decree that you are on the road to recovery and victory.

Remember, your victory needs to be at all costs. Victory, in spite of all terror. Victory, no matter how long and how hard the road may be; for without victory there is no survival! (Winston Churchill)

Stay Prayed Up & Encouraged.

Stand at the crossroads and look; ask for the ancient paths, ask where the good way is, and walk in it, and you will find rest for your souls. (Jeremiah 6:16)

At the end of the day:

___
___
___
___
___
___
___
___
___
___
___

APRIL 14

THE QUESTION?

Can you trust God when things are downright ugly and nasty? Broke, unhappy, loss of job, divorce, heartache and in pain. Would you still trust Him?

Today God wants to see your faith put into action. Do you have faith as small as a mustard seed? (Matthew 17:20)

Remember, it's easy to praise and worship if things are all gravy; but at the end of the day, if you lost it all would you still trust Him?

Do not fear what you are about to suffer. Behold, the devil is about to throw some of you into prison, that you may be tested, and for ten days you will have tribulation. Be faithful unto death, and I will give you the crown of life. (Revelation 2:10)

At the end of the day:

_____
_____
_____
_____
_____
_____
_____
_____
_____
_____
_____

APRIL 15

THE PROCESS

You might have been and are currently in a season of hurt, pain, heartache, rejection and loneliness. Which has made you feel as if you are alone and God has forsaken you.

Today it's time to understand the process to it all. God is still in the trenches with you. Through all the hurt and trauma....it is your reward.

What you think is devastation is really a setup for greatness over your life!

Remember, the process is processing you for something greater than the comfort you were living in before it all got started. (Tera Carissa Hodges)

Blessed is the one who perseveres under trial because, having stood the test, that person will receive the crown of life that the Lord has promised to those who love him. (James 1:12)

At the end of the day:

_____
_____
_____
_____
_____
_____
_____
_____

APRIL 16

IT IS FINISHED...HE HAS RISEN

Today is not about Easter bunnies, baskets of candies and Easter egg hunts. Jesus was crucified on Friday, but on Sunday He Got Up! Let me just say what appears to be dead, will come back to life again! Jesus Christ is alive! He lives and He holds our future!

"And the angel answered and said unto the women, Fear not ye: for I know that ye seek Jesus, which was crucified. He is not here: for he is risen, as he said. Come, see the place where the Lord lay. And go quickly, and tell his disciples that he is risen from the dead; and, behold, he goeth before you into Galilee; there shall ye see him: lo, I have told you." (Matthew 28:5-7)

The Resurrection of Jesus is God's Power. All of us still experience the consequences of sin and deal with relationships, financial, emotional, health and physical needs. We even endure pain and cry over those issues, but we are still VICTORIOUS because of the finished work of Jesus on the Cross for us.

God has promised His Resurrection life and power to all who believe in Jesus! No matter what's going on in your life and the problems and situations that you are facing, always remember that Jesus died for your sins. For every single last one of your sins you committed, you can be healed, forgiven and more importantly you can know the power of His Resurrection to change your life!

But he was wounded for our transgressions, he was bruised for our iniquities: the chastisement of our peace was upon him; and with his stripes we are healed. (Isaiah 53:5)

If you believe in Jesus you have access to that same power through His name and the presence of the Holy Spirit.

At the end of the day:

APRIL 17

THE PAIN EQUALS THE BLESSINGS

It's hard when life throws you some blows. I mean everywhere you turn you are being hit from every single direction. Work woes, marriage woes, relationship woes and sometimes even church woes. Don't get it twisted…. Satan is trying to knock you down to keep you upset and depressed. But God has given you authority to trample on snakes and scorpions. YOU HAVE THE POWER OVER THE ENEMY!!!! (Luke 10:19)

Today recognize the fact that it does hurt and it's not fun when you are going through. But the level of the pain that you are dealing with is an indication of your blessings that God has for you with your name on it!!!

Remember, the sufferings of this present time can't compare to what God has in store for YOU! (Romans 8:18)

We are pressed on every side by troubles, but we are not crushed. We are perplexed, but not driven to despair. We are hunted down, but never abandoned by God. We get knocked down, but we are not destroyed. (2 Corinthians 4:8-10)

At the end of the day:

_____
_____
_____
_____
_____
_____
_____

APRIL 18

THE ORIGINAL GPS

We live in a world now that technology can get us where we need to go. But how many of you know that God is the one that can only get you where you really need to go? It's all good to type in an address to get you from here to there. But you need to realize that every important decision and major life changes come from direct counsel and direction from God Himself.

Today, know that even though you don't know what's ahead of you, God will never leave you nor forsake you. He is always their helping you navigate through life.

I will instruct you and teach you in the way you should go; I will counsel you with my eye upon you. (Psalm 32:8)

At the end of the day:

_____
_____
_____
_____
_____
_____
_____
_____
_____
_____

APRIL 19

THE NEXT THING WILL BE THE BEST THING

The car, house, job, man or woman you have been mourning over doesn't even compare to what the good Lord is about to store upon you. Yeah, what you had was great but your eyes have not seen nor ears have not heard, what God is about to do for you! (1 Corinthians 2:9)

Today don't think about the former things and forget about the past. God is springing forth up something new in your life. (Isaiah 43:18-19) He has seen your tears and knows that you deserve better than that.

Remember, what the devil designed to infect you, will not affect you.

At the end of the day:

APRIL 20

THE LORD WILL STEP RIGHT IN

At the blink of an eye, life can throw you some curve balls that will have you high, low and upside down like a roller coaster. You might be frantic because you don't know what to do; but just at that right moment when you think that you are about to fall to the ground, the Lord will step right in.

Today, you don't have to sweat and worry about the unforeseen. God goes with you 24/7 365 days a year. He will never leave nor forsake you. (Deuteronomy 31:6)

Remember, God will never leave you desolate, broken or alone. The moment that you feel like giving up; He'll step right in and come to your rescue.

So, do not fear, for I am with you; do not be dismayed, for I am your God. I will strengthen you and help you; I will uphold you with my righteous right hand. (Isaiah 41:10)

At the end of the day:

___
___
___
___
___
___
___
___
___

APRIL 21

THE ENERGIZER BUNNY

The Energizer Bunny is known for its advertising tag line, "He keeps going and going" But how many of you keep on going and going? I mean rushing, hurrying, and always telling folks that you gotta go! Is that the story of your life?

Today be still and STOP! Why are you rushing? There is no need for you to keep going and going. When you're rushing and going nonstop, you can rush yourself right in the wrong direction.

Remember, nature does not hurry, yet everything is accomplished. (Lao Tzu)

"Careful planning puts you ahead in the long run, hurry and scurry puts you further behind" (Proverbs 21:5) MSG

At the end of the day:

APRIL 22

THE LORD WILL FIGHT FOR YOU

How many of you are going through a storm right now? A medical report that could be life threatening, on the edge of divorcing, job not working out or someone ducking and diving that owes you money? No matter what the storm you are facing today, you must be still and know The Lord is fighting for you!

Going through a divorce?
The Lord is fighting for YOU, BE STILL.

Can't find a job or lost a job?
The Lord is fighting for YOU, BE STILL.

Someone is mistreating you?
The Lord is fighting for YOU, BE STILL.

Bad medical report?
The Lord is fighting for YOU, BE STILL.

No money in the bank?
The Lord is fighting for YOU, BE STILL.

Tired of folks lying and talking about you?
The Lord is fighting for YOU, BE STILL.

Sick and tired of being sick and tired?
The Lord is fighting for YOU, BE STILL.

Today you will not try to take matters in your own hands, but you will put all your trust in our Heavenly Father. Remember the battle is not yours it belongs to The Lord.

Be still, and know that I am God. (Psalm 46:10)

The Lord will fight for you, and you have only to be silent. (Exodus14:14)

At the end of the day:

APRIL 23

THE ENEMY DOESN'T PLAY FAIR

The thief comes to steal, kill and destroy. (John 10:10) He is literally prowling around like a lion looking for someone to devour; don't let it be you! (1 Pewter 5:8)

Today, be very strong in The Lord and mighty in His power. Put on the full armor of God, so that you can war against the devil's wicked schemes. (Ephesians 6:10-11)

Remember, don't let the devil steal the joy you have. Shake off the negativity he is trying to cover you with, and begin to praise in his face! No matter what. God is still in it!

Stay Prayed Up & Encouraged

Be still, and know that I am God (Psalm 46:10)

At the end of the day:

_____
_____
_____
_____
_____
_____
_____
_____
_____
_____

APRIL 24

THE DEVIL ISN'T IN A RED CAPE

When some people think about the devil, they have a realistic picture of him being dressed in a red cape and pointy horns. But fact is the devil/enemy could be your spouse, friend, coworker and sometimes even your child. He disguises himself as an angel of light to get at you. (2 Corinthians 11:14) For you to win, you must be sober-minded, watchful and alert because the devil prowls around just like a roaring lion looking for someone to devour. (1 Peter 5:8) Don't let it be you!!!

Put on the whole armor of God today so that you may be able to stand against the schemes of the devil. You are not wrestling against flesh and blood, but against the spiritual forces of evil in heavenly places. (Ephesians 6:11-12)

Every day it is imperative for you to submit yourselves to God and constantly resist the devil. When you do, he will flee from you!!! (James 4:7)

The devil who deceived them was thrown into the lake of fire and sulfur, where the beast and the false prophet were. They will be tortured day and night, forever and ever. (Revelation 20:10)

Stay Prayed Up & Encouraged ~

At the end of the day:

_____
_____
_____
_____
_____

APRIL 25

THE DEVIL HAS A PLOT BUT GOD HAS A PLAN

The enemy comes to kill and destroy. (John 10:10) Taking you out is his priority. Although he may be plotting evil schemes and plans for you, he will not succeed! (Psalm 21:11)

Today know that there are many plans in the mind of a man, but it is the purpose of the Lord that will stand. (Proverbs 19:21)

Remember, the enemy doesn't have the final say, God does.

You will triumph!

That people may know, from the rising of the sun and from the west, that there is none besides me; I am the Lord, and there is no other. I form light and create darkness, I make well-being and create calamity, I am the Lord, who does all these things. (Isaiah 45:6-7)

At the end of the day:

_____
_____
_____
_____
_____
_____
_____
_____
_____
_____
_____
_____

APRIL 26

THE DEVIL DIDN'T DESTROY YOU

As much as the enemy tried and tried to take you down and out.... He still didn't succeed. God is fighting on your behalf!

Today you need to know that the enemy might think that they are doing something. (let them keep thinking that) But The Lord is defeating your enemies who are coming at you; to be defeated right in front of your very own eyes. They might come from the West but they will flee from the East. (Deuteronomy 28:7)

Remember, satan targets your mind. His weapon is lies. His purpose is to make you ignorant of God's will. But your defense is inspired by The Word of God. You have to confuse the enemy!

So, the next time you start to worry.... just begin to worship instead....and the enemy will flee from you!!!! (James 4:7)

Humble yourselves, therefore, under God's mighty hand, that he may lift you up in due time. (1 Peter 5:6)

At the end of the day:

_____
_____
_____
_____
_____
_____
_____
_____
_____
_____

APRIL 27

THE DESIRES OF YOUR HEART

Do you have a dream so big in your heart that you haven't told anyone about? They are the dreams that are so big that it seems impossible for you to accomplish it. Those dreams are from God and He wants you to step out on Faith and trust Him.

Today, if you know that there is something in your heart that you are believing God to work on your behalf...all you have to do is stand in Faith and don't give up. He knows the desires of your heart, and will finish what He started. Hold on!

Delight yourself in the Lord, and he will give you the desires of your heart. (Psalm 37:4)

At the end of the day:

APRIL 28

THE ATTACK WILL COME TO AN END

The trouble, trial and storm that you are in has been hard. If folks really knew what you were going through they could understand why you wanted to quit.... But the devil is a lie! Because you know all attacks will come to an end.

Today you can rejoice because you have suffered for quite a while and the death date to your trial has come to an end. You may have been weeping throughout the nights...but God says your joy is coming. (Psalm 30:5)

Remember, every attack is limited in duration. (Bishop Dale C. Bonner)

All who rage against you will surely be ashamed and disgraced; those who oppose you will be as nothing and perish (Isaiah 41:11)

But suddenly, your ruthless enemies will be crushed like the finest of dust. Your many attackers will be driven away like chaff before the wind. Suddenly, in an instant, (Isaiah 29:5)

At the end of the day:

_____
_____
_____
_____
_____
_____
_____

APRIL 29

THANK GOD FOR THE PRESSURE

Some days you are probably asking yourself, "How in the world are you going to make it through this day?" There are days that you just have to Thank God that you made it to work and back home. You are in such a daze that you have no idea how you even drove a car, signs of wonders and miracles of how the bills are getting paid or how food got on the table. And the biggest of them all, how you still have your mind. It's amazing how you are not in a white straight jacket rocking back and forth in a padded cell. The pressure of life's issues has overtaken you and you feel like you don't have a clue on what to do next.

But Thank God for a man named Jesus, because today you are going to Thank Him for your pressure. The pressure that you are in He is getting ready to use it to thrust and take you farther than you've ever been before. So, don't get so caught up in your circumstances that you miss your blessings. Give Him praise in the midst of the storm.

Remember, if you are under pressure in your life. Know that God is with you 24/7 to comfort and see you through. He will never leave nor forsake YOU!

Blessed is the man who remains steadfast under trial, for when he has stood the test he will receive the crown of life, which God has promised to those who love him. (James 1:12)

At the end of the day:

_____

_____

_____

_____

APRIL 30

TELL YOURSELF

Life and death are in the power of the tongue. (Proverbs 18:21) What you say has merit. So be careful of what you speak.

Today, no matter how bad you don't want to get up, tell yourself...

> I can make it!
> I can do it!
> It's hard,
>
> But I'm pressing!
> I've cried my last tear!
> I can get past this hurt!
> God loves me too much to leave me like this!
> I believe everything that The Lord has said about my life!
> I'm believing it just got better and God is fixing it!!!

Remember, the tongue is a small thing; but what enormous damage can it do! (James 3:5)

For by your words you will be acquitted, and by your words you will be condemned. (Matthew 12:37)

At the end of the day:

_____
_____
_____
_____
_____
_____

MAY 1

TALK LIKE YOU KNOW

You might have had some hard knocks in your life, but that doesn't mean that you should just roll over and take it. God says you are victorious and you are more than a conqueror! (1 Corinthians 15:57 & Romans 8:37)

Today you need to talk like you know who you belong too.

> Talk like you are victorious!
> Talk like God reigns!
> Talk like God has called the fight and said YOU win!
> Talk like YOU are the head and not the tail!
> Talk like YOU know who is fighting this battle!

Remember, "Wise words bring approval, but fools are destroyed by their own words." (Ecclesiastes 10:12)

Do not let any unwholesome talk come out of your mouths, but only what is helpful for building others up according to their needs, that it may benefit those who listen. (Ephesians 4:29)

Stay Prayed Up & Encouraged and Talk Like YOU KNOW!

At the end of the day:

___
___
___
___
___
___

MAY 2

TAKING OUT THE TRASH

It is important to be watchful and sober-minded daily. The devil is prowling around like a fierce roaring lion looking for someone to devour and get a hold of. (1 Peter 5:8) Don't let it be you!

Today is the day that you are going to empty the trash and remove the negativity and garbage out of your life. The devil is a lie!!! You are NOT crazy, bipolar, depressed, losing your mind and you, for sure, are not a victim because of what someone did to you. You are more than a conqueror through Christ who loves you. (Romans 8:37)

Remember, the devil had a plot, but God had a plan!

Stay prayed up and encouraged, this too shall pass.

Put on the whole armor of God, that you may be able to stand against the schemes of the devil. (Ephesians 6:11)

At the end of the day:

_____
_____
_____
_____
_____
_____
_____
_____
_____
_____
_____

MAY 3

SWING BATTER BATTER SWING

Often when life throws you a curve ball; you stay so focused on the damage that the ball caused, that you can't see the blessing(s) that God has just sent you. But know HE causes everything to work together for the good of those who love Him and are called according to His purpose. (Romans 8:28)

Today don't be so fixated on the ball that life has hit you with, but let God swing back for you. He is in this and fighting for you. (Exodus 14:14) Yes, the ball has hit and landed, but God is in the game with you. (Isaiah 41:10)

Remember, the enemy might have the bat…. but you are ballin with Jesus!

You shall eat in plenty and be satisfied, and praise the name of the Lord your God, who has dealt wondrously with you. And my people shall never again be put to shame. (Joel 2:26)

At the end of the day:

_____
_____
_____
_____
_____
_____
_____
_____
_____

MAY 4

SURRENDER

A lot of times when things aren't going our way it's easy to want to blame God because we cry and pray out to Him and say, "God why are you allowing this to happen?" But the problem is we keep getting involved and we're not turning it over to Him to do what He needs to do.

Today is the day that you surrender it all over to The Lord. You are getting in the way of God, truly fixing what needs to be fixed. If you could just step back and release it over; God will take care of it.

Remember, you have to surrender to what is. Let go to what was, and have the faith to what will be (Sonia Ricotti)

Every word of God proves true. He is a shield to all who come to him for protection. (Proverbs 30:5)

At the end of the day:

_____
_____
_____
_____
_____
_____
_____
_____
_____
_____

MAY 5

STUCK

There comes a time in life where you are going to have to suck it up and just move on. The pain, hurt, despair, and turmoil can be much to bear. And God doesn't want you down, depressed....and definitely not stuck on someone or somewhere that He is trying to elevate you from.

Today, know that it is easy to remain in what you know. But until you turn it over to The Lord and truly trust Him....you will be stuck!

Remember, growth is painful and change is painful. But nothing is as painful as staying stuck where you don't belong. (Mandy Hale)

Forget the former things; do not dwell on the past. See, I am doing a new thing! Now it springs up; do you not perceive it? I am making a way in the wilderness and streams in the wasteland. (Isaiah 43:18-19)

At the end of the day:

_____
_____
_____
_____
_____
_____
_____
_____
_____
_____

MAY 6

STRONGER, BETTER AND BRIGHTER

A baby must crawl before he or she walks; and just like a baby you have grown day by day. Without even realizing it you have gotten stronger and better, because of it brighter days are ahead.

Today, say thank you God! Because what the enemy meant for evil, God is getting ready to work it out for your good. (Genesis 50:20)

Remember, you are God's child and there is nothing that you can't overcome!

Stay Prayed Up & Encouraged ~

Although they plot against you, their evil schemes will never succeed. (Psalm 21:11)

At the end of the day:

_____
_____
_____
_____
_____
_____
_____
_____
_____
_____
_____
_____

MAY 7

STRENGTH WITHIN

God wants to increase your strength and the power to overcome any difficulties, trials or storms that you are facing today. He wants to make you a man or a woman as strong as steel. Keep believing and standing in Faith and God will give you a victorious supernatural strength to defeat any obstacle at your door.

I can do all things through Christ which strengthens me. (Philippians 4:13)

At the end of the day:

MAY 8

STOP! THE FEAR IS GONE

As soon as you get the courage to step out on Faith, satan starts talking in your ear and before you know it you are back-peddling and fear starts taking over your mind. In the Bible, it says that fear is a spirit. Fear ultimately tries to hold us back and plays on our emotions.

Today, know that you have power over fear! Believe God's Word and walk into the Victory that he has prepared for you!

For God hath not given us the spirit of fear; but of power, and of love, and of a sound mind. (2 Timothy 1: 7)

At the end of the day:

_____
_____
_____
_____
_____
_____
_____
_____
_____
_____
_____
_____
_____
_____

MAY 9

STOP! NOW JUST LET GOD

I know that you want to try to fix it and work it out on your own, but I promise you that is not the way you need to go. If you truly want to have victory and the Crown of Life you are going to have to give your worries and cares over to The Lord because He does care for you. (1 Peter 5:7)

I've never seen the righteous forsaken or God's children begging for bread. (Psalm 37:25) Now you have seen the outcome when you have tried to fix it. So today give God a try and let Him work it out for you. He will never fail you.

Now when these things begin to take place, stand up and lift up your heads, because your deliverance is approaching. (Luke 21:28)

At the end of the day:

_____
_____
_____
_____
_____
_____
_____
_____
_____
_____
_____
_____

MAY 10

STICKS & STONES MAY BREAK MY BONES... BUT GOD REIGNS IN ME

In life people might try to hurt you, some might think that they are getting the best of you, others might think that they are destroying you...I've come to learn that people get pleasure in putting others down.... BUT TODAY IS THE DAY TO REMIND YOU.... YOU ARE A CHILD OF THE MOST HIGH GOD!

Yet to all who did receive him, to those who believed in His name, He gave the right to become children of God (John 1:12)

We all eventually age, gray hairs come about, weight comes upon, some lose hair. God says, "Even to your old age and gray hairs I am He, I am He who will sustain you. I have made you and I will carry you; I will sustain you and I will rescue you." (Isaiah 46:4)

When condemning voices destroy your self-image, simply look in the mirror and know that you are approved by Almighty God!

Your beauty should not come from outward adornment, such as elaborate hairstyles and the wearing of gold jewelry or fine clothes. Rather, it should be that of your inner self, the unfading beauty of a gentle and quiet spirit, which is of great worth in God's sight. (1 Peter 3:3, 4)

What God knows about me is infinitely more important.

At the end of the day:

_____

_____

_____

_____

May 11
STICK & TOUGH IT OUT

A lot of people feel as if it is easier said than done when you are going through to just, "stick and tough it out." Fact is God needs to see that you are faithful and no matter how the winds may blow and how big and bad the enemy appears… you still need to know where your help comes from. (Psalm 121:2)

Today, be like a tree planted that is unmovable. No matter how big and mighty the enemy huffs, puffs and tries to blow and take you down…YOU WILL NOT BEND OR BREAK! (Jeremiah 17:8)

Remember, tough times don't last, but tough people do! The beginning is always tough…but once you are in it YOU WILL become unstoppable!!!

YOU can get through this!

Stay Prayed Up & Encouraged ~

In every way we're troubled but not crushed, frustrated but not in despair, persecuted but not abandoned, struck down but not destroyed. (2 Corinthians 4:8-9)

At the end of the day:

_____
_____
_____
_____
_____
_____

MAY 12

STEPPING OUT

Sometimes when things don't go our way we start to blame God and question what He is doing in our lives. You have to know that God moves when you move.

Today, do you part so God can start moving and working things out in your life. But first you have to step out on Faith. Scripture tells us that we just need a little Faith as small as a mustard seed. Quit being scared and anxious because He did not put those thoughts and feelings in you; and step out on a leap of Faith and watch Him move in your life.

And without faith it is impossible to please Him, for whoever would draw near to God must believe that He exists and that He rewards those who seek Him. (Hebrews 11:6)

At the end of the day:

___
___
___
___
___
___
___
___
___
___
___
___

MAY 13

STEPPING OUT ON FAITH

It's no secret that my marriage didn't work and it devastated me. I couldn't believe that at one point of my life I was on top and in the blink of an eye my twin teenage boys and two teacup Yorkies were literally homeless. We had to go back to Kentucky with nothing but our clothes. Talk about a depression. I was 21 years old when I built my home for me and my sons, and to stay place to place with your kids is so heartbreaking. But deep inside I knew God wasn't going to leave me there.

I hear all the time, "Do I have regrets?" I used to, until God showed me that He was going to use my tragedy to bless others. I would have never written a devotional and met so many beautiful people had I not gone through that storm. I stepped out on Faith because God told me to go. Despite what family and friends were saying and the names they called me, I still followed God.

In life, things don't turn out the way you expect and it can hurt. You can ask God why are you doing this to me? You can be mad at the person that has done evil to you, or you can pray and ask God to give you wisdom and direction over your situation. You must continue to be faithful and wait for God to tell you what to do.

God will avenge every wrong in your life that has been done to you. It might not happen when you want it... but it will happen.

Continue to step out on Faith, no matter what lies ahead. If you ask God, He will tell you what to do. Trust and believe that nothing He will do is meant to harm you.

Trust in the Lord with all your heart, and do not lean on your own understanding. In all your ways, acknowledge him, and he will make straight your paths. (Proverbs 3:5-6)

At the end of the day:

MAY 14

STEP

Sometimes in life you must step out of your comfort zone and let God move and work in your life.

Today you need to step and praise your way through. Just walk right into your new season and victory!

Remember, God is not attracted to your problems, but He is attracted to your praise!!! Now Get to Stepping!!!!

Look, I have given you authority over all the power of the enemy, and you can walk among snakes and scorpions and crush them. Nothing will injure you. (Luke 10:19)

At the end of the day:

MAY 15

STAY

It's easy to get off track because of the trials and storms that have come your way. But God has called you victorious... so you must continue to stand and stay!

Today don't get focused on what you are dealing with, but get focused on who you have to deal with them...GOD! So, no matter what is being thrown your way, God has already called the fight and said, YOU WIN!!!! All you have to do is trust Him and not lean on your own understanding. (Proverbs 3:5)

Remember, stay in Faith, stay with God, stay prayed up, stay in your Word, stay encouraged and stay pressing toward the goal for the prize of the upward call of God in Christ Jesus! (Philippians 3:14)

But seek first the kingdom of God and his righteousness, and all these things will be added to you. (Matthew 6:33)

At the end of the day:

_____
_____
_____
_____
_____
_____
_____
_____
_____
_____

MAY 16

STAY FAITHFUL

Life can take a toll on us. It's easy to want to throw in the towel and say, "I give up" but that's not what God wants to see you do.

Today, remember that you are God's child. He knows about every single thing that you are facing and going through at this moment. But He wants to see how you are dealing with it. Are you being faithful and trusting Him to work it out, or have you gotten to the place that you're angry and mad because you think nothing is happening on your behalf?

Don't give up! Continue to serve God, give Him praise and do the right thing. He is watching and... before you know it...your breakthrough and turnaround will be right at your door.

And let us not grow weary of doing good, for in due season we will reap, if we do not give up. (Galatians 6:9)

At the end of the day:

_____
_____
_____
_____
_____
_____
_____
_____
_____
_____

MAY 17

STARTING OVER

Don't be afraid to start over. God will never put more on you than you can bear. The changes and challenges may be hard, but He will provide a way for you to endure. (1 Corinthians 10:13)

Today, give all worries and anxieties over to The Lord. God doesn't give you the spirit of fear - but of power, love and self-control. (2 Timothy 1:7) Have confidence that you are getting ready to walk into the best days of your life!

Remember, don't be afraid to start over. It's a chance to build something better this time around.

Forget the former things; do not dwell on the past. See, I am doing a new thing! Now it springs up; do you not perceive it? I am making a way in the wilderness and streams in the wasteland. (Isaiah 43:18-19)

At the end of the day:

MAY 18

STAND TALL

The Bible tells us that our enemies come to kill and destroy. (John 10:10) They will even try to attack you but The Lord will conquer you from them from one direction and they will flee from you seven. (Deuteronomy 28:7)

Today God needs you to stand tall. You may not recognize it, but despite all that you are going through you are still strong. So, don't be afraid of those coming for you, because God is with you. (Deuteronomy 31:6)

Remember, though you walk in the midst of troubles, trials and a storm; God is still preserving your life. His hand is stretched out to your enemies and He WILL deliver YOU from them! (Psalm 138:7)

Therefore, take up the whole armor of God, that you may be able to withstand in the evil day, and having done all, to stand firm. (Ephesians 6:13)

At the end of the day:

_____
_____
_____
_____
_____
_____
_____
_____
_____

MAY 19

STAND FIRM

The enemy wants you, it's a fact. You must be aware and alert at all times. He is prowling around like a roaring lion on the hunt for fresh prey, and if you are not careful he will get you. (1 Peter 5:8)

Today and moving forward be on guard and stand firm in your faith. You are strong and courageous even if you don't feel it. (1 Corinthians 16:13) God has not given you a spirit of fear and timidity, but of power, love, and self-discipline. (2 Timothy 1:7)

When you awake and before you even step out of your bed put on the full armor of God, so that you will be able to stand firm against the schemes of the devil. (Ephesians 6:11)

Remember, stand firm and hold to the traditions which you were taught. (2 Thessalonians 2:15)

Above all, you must live as citizens of heaven, conducting yourselves in a manner worthy of the Good News about Christ. Then, whether I come and see you again or only hear about you, I will know that you are standing together with one spirit and one purpose, fighting together for the faith, which is the Good News. (Philippians 1:27)

At the end of the day:

_____
_____
_____
_____
_____
_____

MAY 20

STAND BACK UP

When you're enduring a storm, sometimes the enemy will use every trick and scheme to knock you down. You must be alert so you can take a stand against the devil. (1 Peter 5:8)

Today no matter how many times you get knocked know that The Lord is right there to lift and pick you back up. (James 4:10)

Remember, when you have prayed and cried, and cried and prayed; just stand and watch the deliverance of The Lord.

It was for freedom that Christ set us free; therefore, keep standing firm and do not be subject again to a yoke of slavery. (Galatians 5:1)

At the end of the day:

_____
_____
_____
_____
_____
_____
_____
_____
_____
_____
_____
_____
_____
_____
_____

MAY 21

SO WHAT

So what if they ended the relationship, let you go from that job or you missed the business opportunity. At the end of the day God has something better in store. You must learn to let closed doors stay closed!

Today don't trip over spilled milk because God has something better in mind for us; (Hebrews 11:40) and the devil knows it and he wants it. So, take up the full armor of God, for when the evil time comes you will be able to resist the enemy; and after the battle you will still be standing firm.

Remember, God Always Keeps His Promises!

Let us hold tightly without wavering to the hope we affirm, for God can be trusted to keep his promise. (Hebrews 10:23)

At the end of the day:

_____
_____
_____
_____
_____
_____
_____
_____
_____
_____
_____
_____

MAY 22

SIT BACK & WATCH THE SHOW

Do not take revenge, my dear friends, but leave room for God's wrath, for it is written: "It is mine to avenge; I will repay," says The Lord. (Romans 12: 19)

There are enemies that say and do things that try to take you out... But you must remember what they say and try to do to you, God will make it where it will backfire on them! So, sit back and watch the show.

"Do not be deceived: God cannot be mocked. A man reaps what he sows." (Galatians 6:7)

I know it's hard to want revenge and fire back when someone hurts and says something that cuts you to the core. But let me remind you...YOU ARE GOD's CHILD & YOU ARE BEAUTIFUL & WONDROUSLY MADE!! Be handcuffed to the Father, because when you are...that ugly sheep in wolves' clothing can't say ANYTHING to hurt you...WHY? Because you are wrapped up in your Father's arms!!!!!!

If you say, "The Lord is my refuge," and you make the Most High your dwelling, no harm will overtake you, no disaster will come near your tent. (Psalm 91: 9-10)

At the end of the day:

___
___
___
___
___

MAY 23

SICK & TIRED OF BEING SICK & TIRED

"Put on the whole armor of God, that ye may be able to stand against the wiles of the devil. Wherefore take unto you the whole armor of God that ye may be able to withstand in the evil day, and having done all, to stand." (Ephesians 6:11, 13)

Family and friends, the title of my Devotional today is just simply how I feel in a nutshell. I went through a lot last year and, like any strong woman in Christ, I am strong; but I can break some days too. Lord knows the devil tries to test me. Through this year, faithfully I have talked about putting on the full armor of God daily before you get ready to walk out that door, because Satan literally is walking around like a roaring lion to see whom he can devour, so you must be ready!!! The more Devotionals I write and the work I do for my home church, I feel I get attacked more and more. I've come to learn though not to give in to the devil!!!!!! I have got to shout and praise, even in the midst of the storm.

"By him, therefore let us offer the sacrifice of praise to God continually, that is, the fruit of our lips giving thanks to his name." (Hebrews 13:15)

I'm not the only one that gets sick and tired of everyday life trials. Some of you are dealing with struggles in your jobs, with your kids, in your marriages, finances, health and so on. I'm here to tell you today that although you might be just like me, sick and tired some days, God is never too sick and tired to pull you through!!! I urge you to cry out to The Lord no matter what your circumstance is. God can hear every single prayer and can wipe every single one of your tears!!! No matter what adverse circumstance, negative situation, or painful condition that is at your doorstep; God Has It!!!!!!!!

This world we live in can be mighty cruel and life can be very hard.

There are going to be good days and bad. There are challenges and disappointments all around. They can be related to your relationships, finances, jobs, health, marriages, families, or friends. But the one thing I can tell you for sure is that the help of God's grace and strength, and the joy of His presence in your life will help you achieve victory over any obstacle that you are encountering today!

At the end of the day:

MAY 24

SHUT UP & PRAY

When life gets real dirty and ugly, do you still trust God? Well Christ is the same yesterday, today and forever. (Hebrews 13:8) He knows what you are going through and has front row tickets to your show. He knows because He knew you before you were even born. (Jeremiah 1:5)

Today, in spite of what you are going through and what it looks like, He needs you to shut up and pray! There are times that you know you have done all that you can; so, the only thing left to do is to bow your head and a have a little talk with Jesus.

Remember, He hears all of your cries. So, continue to pray to God for help and this too shall pass! (Psalm 18:6)

But God has surely listened and has heard my prayer. (Psalm 66:19)

At the end of the day:

_____
_____
_____
_____
_____
_____
_____
_____
_____
_____
_____
_____

MAY 25

SHOW UP FOR GOD & HE WILL SHOW OUT FOR YOU

If you are going through and you feel like you have prayed, cried out to The Lord and kept standing for your miracle and breakthrough, you must ask yourself are you truly showing up for Him?

Today it's time to quit playing and really spend time with God. He wants to know that you are committed and really trust Him. It's one thing to know scriptures, but it's another when you know what it means to weep for a night and He brought you joy in the morning. (Psalm 30:5)

Remember if you show up for God, He will show out for you!!!

Understand, therefore, that the LORD your God is indeed God. He is the faithful God who keeps his covenant for a thousand generations and lavishes his unfailing love on those who love him and obey his commands. (Deuteronomy 7:9)

At the end of the day:

_____
_____
_____
_____
_____
_____
_____
_____
_____

MAY 26

SHOUT

The enemy loves to see you sweat. He comes for you with such power and force, like a roaring lion looking for someone to devour. (1 Peter 5:8) Are you prepared to fight him?

Today and moving forward you need to shout and praise in advance, while the storms are raging in your life. The best way to defeat the enemy is to get your praise on, when the situation is looking bleak. The enemy wants to keep you depressed, in sin and he wants your mind. Well, the devil is a lie and you will not fall for his tricks and schemes. Right now, put on the whole armor of God, that you may be able to stand against the schemes of the devil. (Ephesians 6:11)

Remember, the enemy wants you to close your mouth, but you are going to "SHOUT" until your victory is won!

For we do not wrestle against flesh and blood, but against the rulers, against the authorities, against the cosmic powers over this present darkness, against the spiritual forces of evil in the heavenly places. (Ephesians 6:12)

At the end of the day:

_____
_____
_____
_____
_____
_____
_____
_____

MAY 27

SHHHHHH & LISTEN

Here I am! I stand at the door and knock. If anyone hears my voice and opens the door, I will come in and eat with that person, and they with me. (Revelation 3:20)

"If only I could handle this myself or if this could just happen it will fix my situation." "I don't know what to do." "I need someone to talk too." How many of you have said something similar or the same thing a time or two? I know I used too. If you have ever tried to handle something on your own without seeking God's guidance and voice, the situation, no matter what it is, it has a way of coming back at you bigger and harder because you tried to do it on your own without Hearing from God.

My sheep hear my voice, and I know them, and they follow me: And I give unto them eternal life; and they shall never perish, neither shall any man pluck them out of my hand. My Father, which gave them me, is greater than all; and no man is able to pluck them out of my Father's hand. I and my Father are one." (John 10:27-30)

At the end of the day:

_____
_____
_____
_____
_____
_____
_____
_____

MAY 28

SEEK HIM FIRST

Today, take time for God at the start of your morning, not just today but every day. Don't give Him what's left of your time. Make Him part of your every morning routine. He is your FIRST priority! Seek Him first and He will do that exceedingly and abundantly on your behalf.

But seek ye first the kingdom of God, and his righteousness; and all these things shall be added unto you. (Matthew 6:33)

At the end of the day:

_____
_____
_____
_____
_____
_____
_____
_____
_____
_____
_____
_____
_____
_____

MAY 29

YOU GOT THIS

There is nothing that is going in your life that is too hard for God. Whether you know it or not...you got this! You're making it and you're fighting. The devil won't and can't win this battle. God has already called you victorious.

Today, you can tell the devil to back on up because you're here to stay. It doesn't matter if he comes from the North, South, East or West...you still will be unmovable. God has given you the strength to overcome. So, therefore, you can take the fiery darts that he throws.

Remember, you have the good fight of Faith in you so you can take what comes your way!!!

I have fought the good fight, I have finished the race, I have kept the faith. Now there is in store for me the crown of righteousness, which the Lord, the righteous Judge, will award to me on that day and not only to me, but also to all who have longed for his appearing. (2 Timothy 4:7-8)

At the end of the day:

_____
_____
_____
_____
_____
_____
_____
_____

MAY 30

SEE NO EVIL, HEAR NO EVIL

There are people in your life that want to drive you crazy. They have you feeling as if you are in a ring with Iron Mike Tyson because you are taking hits like a champion prize fighter. You must know that is nothing but the enemy, and he wouldn't be fighting so hard or coming for you if he didn't know the blessing(s) that God has for your life.

Today I want you to stop acknowledging and listening to lies of the enemy. Satan can't outsmart you because you are aware of his evil schemes. (2 Corinthians 2:11) Just continue to submit yourselves to God and resist the devil and he will flee from you. (James 4:7)

Remember, confuse the devil and praise now in your storm; and watch the breakthrough that God will release for YOU!

Finally, be strong in the Lord and in his mighty power. Put on the full armor of God, so that you can take your stand against the devil's schemes. (Ephesians 6:10-11)

At the end of the day:

_____
_____
_____
_____
_____
_____
_____
_____

MAY 31

RUN TO GOD

I know that life can get hard and sometimes you just don't know what to do. You start to wear down other people's ears with your problems. Instead of running all over town trying to get others' advice on what to do, you need to be running to God for dear life. Your true and only source!

Today before you text, call and get in your car to go to tell someone what you're going through, run to God and seek after Him. His streets, roads and highways stretch out just for YOU...and He will make your path straight! (Proverbs 3:6)

God will make you finish this race strong and as the winner! (2 Timothy 4:7)

For the pagans run after all these things, and your heavenly Father knows that you need them. But seek first his kingdom and his righteousness, and all these things will be given to you as well. (Matthew 6:32-33)

At the end of the day:

_____
_____
_____
_____
_____
_____
_____
_____

JUNE 1

RISE UP

The enemy no longer has you. A lot of you might need to hear that again...I said, "THE ENEMY NO LONGER HAS YOU!" Whatever grip he had over your life, health, marriage, child, finances, career or body are destroyed in the name of Jesus!

Today, you will rise up and take victory over your life. You will no longer be a victim, but you will be a VICTOR. God says, "That he has plans to give you a future and hope. Not for demise. (Jeremiah 29:11) Your future is bright and beautiful. Every single one of God's promises for your life is coming to pass.

Satan's Schemes We Don't Acknowledge or Play Into!

God shall arise, His enemies shall be scattered; and those who hate Him shall flee before Him (Psalm 68:1)

At the end of the day:

_____
_____
_____
_____
_____
_____
_____
_____
_____
_____

JUNE 2

RIGHT ON TIME

"We all at some point have heard, God is never late, but always on time." Fact is God showed up when

Shadrach, Meshach and Abednego got thrown into the fiery furnace. (Daniel 3:23-25) He showed up when Daniel was thrown in the Lion's Den. (Daniel 6:16-22) He was right there with Joseph in prison and gave him favor. (Genesis 39:21) So what makes you think that He can't rescue you in your trial/storm?

Today you need to know that God shows up when you need Him the most. He is never late and knows when He is needed. He is not going to go off of your time...but He will go off of His time. What feels like it is killing you is really God stretching you. You have to trust Him and know that He knows what He is doing. God has said, "He will never leave YOU." (Joshua 1:5)

Remember, God shows up in the midst of trouble not the absence. He WILL step in right on time!

Indeed, the LORD is the one who will keep on walking in front of you. He'll be with you and won't leave you or abandon you, so never be afraid and never be dismayed. (Deuteronomy 31:8)

At the end of the day:

_____
_____
_____
_____
_____
_____

JUNE 3

YOU CAN'T FOOL A SEED

How many of you are walking around being nice, kind, and generous to those around you? And how many of you are being nasty, wicked, evil and surly to folks?

Don't get it twisted. God can't be mocked. For whatever you sow, you will reap. (Galatians 6:7) So, be careful of the seed that you are throwing down.

Remember you can't fool a seed. It already knows the assignment Regardless of what you name it, it will produce after its kind (Hart Ramsey)

The point is this, *Whoever sows sparingly will also reap sparingly, and whoever sows bountifully will also reap bountifully.*

At the end of the day:

_____

_____

_____

_____

_____

_____

_____

_____

_____

_____

JUNE 4

REJOICING, RESTORATION & RESTITUTION

God is God! And He is nothing like a man that He shall lie. If He said it, you can best believe that it is going to come to pass. (Numbers 23:19)

Today it's time for rejoicing, restoration and restitution due. God has seen your tears flow. Yes, even He is hurting and your faithfulness when you could have acted a fool. He said that vengeance was His and He would repay. (Deuteronomy 32:35) He is working this thing out for you!

Remember, God is on a rescue mission on your behalf. He is recovering everything that was lost, stolen and broken.

What God can do for you will override anything anyone else has done to you! (Joyce Meyer)

Do not take revenge, my dear friends, but leave room for God's wrath, for it is written: "It is mine to avenge; I will repay," says the Lord. (Romans 12:19)

At the end of the day:

_____
_____
_____
_____
_____
_____
_____
_____

JUNE 5

REJOICE IN TRIBULATION

Everyone in this world will have tribulation of some sort. The good news is that God has said that in Him we will have peace. He knows that there will be tribulation, but be of good courage because He has overcome the world. (John16:33)

Today keep God's commands and endure patiently. When you do He will keep you from the hour of trial that is going to come on the whole world to test those. (Revelation 3:10)

Remember, after you have suffered a little while, the God of all grace, who has called you to his eternal glory in Christ, will Himself restore, confirm, strengthen, and establish you. (1 Peter 5:10)

We can rejoice, too, when we run into problems and trials, for we know that they help us develop endurance. And endurance develops strength of character, and character strengthens our confident hope of salvation. (Romans 5:3-4)

At the end of the day:

_____
_____
_____
_____
_____
_____
_____
_____
_____

JUNE 6

REJOICE EVEN WHEN

The enemy can come at you so strong that it feels as if Hurricane Katrina has hit your life. But no matter what you.... still have to rejoice in the chaos!

Today with all the turmoil that you have been dealing with, you still have to praise God in it and through it.

Remember, suffering is part of our training program for becoming wise. (Ram Dass)

So be truly glad. There is wonderful joy ahead, even though you have to endure many trials for a little while. (1 Peter 1:6)

At the end of the day:

_____
_____
_____
_____
_____
_____
_____
_____
_____
_____
_____
_____
_____
_____

JUNE 7

REDIRECTED

Often when people are rejected they start to focus on the rejection rather than the redirection that God is shifting them too.

Today, thank God for your rejection because they just set you up for bigger and better. It's imperative that we learn to be grateful for closed doors!

Remember, you may feel as if your whole world is falling apart because you just got rejected. But just know that this is God's way of showing you that things are falling into place!

Stay Prayed Up & Encouraged

Whoever listens to you listens to me; whoever rejects you rejects me; but whoever rejects me rejects him who sent me. (Luke 10:16)

At the end of the day:

_____
_____
_____
_____
_____
_____
_____
_____
_____
_____

JUNE 8

RECOVERY TIME

You may have lost someone or something. But God says it's time to forget about the former things and start to think about what lies ahead. (Isaiah 43:18)

Today, stop looking back at yesterday and look forward to what God has for you now and to come. You need to know that God is doing a new thing and He is making a way. Just believe! (Isaiah 43:19)

Remember, it's recovery time! Everything that was taken, stolen or lost will be restored!

Forgetting what lies behind and reaching forward to what lies ahead, (Philippians 3:13)

At the end of the day:

_____
_____
_____
_____
_____
_____
_____
_____
_____
_____
_____
_____

JUNE 9

QUIT LOOKING AT THE NEGATIVE

Often times when your back is up against a wall and you feel like you have nowhere to turn, your situation can look bleak. I mean, let's face it if you are looking at it with carnal eyes; it looks as if there is no way that you are coming out of this. All you can see is the negative and the inconvenience that is being caused in your life. And from the looks of things, it doesn't appear that much is in your favor. But little does the enemy know that you are handcuffed to a man named Jesus and that is your favor.

Today, I want you to erase and put away all negative thoughts and realize that is no one but satan trying to get your mind. Despite how it looks, God is still fighting your battle. It's not over yet!

So, rest easy and think positive. Don't give into the enemies' traps. God is still on the throne!

And let us not grow weary of doing good, for in due season, we will reap, if we do not give up. (Galatians 6:9)

At the end of the day:

_____
_____
_____
_____
_____
_____
_____
_____
_____

JUNE 10

PUSHED INTO YOUR PURPOSE

The things that you are going through right now might have you thinking that God is punishing you or He is not hearing your prayers. Those thoughts are not from God but of the enemy to play tricks in your head. He doesn't want you to follow and listen to the Word from The Lord.

Today and moving forward know that God is doing a new thing in you. He already knows how your story will end. He is pushing you toward your purpose in life. Sometimes the very thing that you think is a punishment is a blessing in disguise.

Remember, if God closes a door, know He is doing that because it's time for you to move forward. He knows you won't move unless circumstances force you too!

Have a Blessed Week Children of God, and Stay Prayed Up & Encouraged!

When he opens doors, no one will be able to close them; when he closes doors, no one will be able to open them. (Isaiah 22:22)

At the end of the day:

_____
_____
_____
_____
_____
_____
_____

JUNE 11

PRESS, PUSH & PRAY

Everyday life challenges can take its toll on a person. But Psalm 37:25 tells us that "the righteous are never forsaken or begging for bread." Real soldiers of The Lord know what to do when attacked. Do you?

Today, you must study and get to know God's Word. Live it & Breathe it! Let it be your daily routine and lifeline. When life is getting rough you must continue to press on. When you think you can't press on any further you must push on. When you think you can't push on you must go into prayer and ask God to help you carry on.

Press, Push and Pray Your Way Through!!!! God is by Your Side!!!

Fear not, for I am with you; be not dismayed, for I am your God; I will strengthen you, I will help you, I will uphold you with my righteous right hand. (Isaiah 41:10)

At the end of the day:

___
___
___
___
___
___
___
___
___
___

JUNE 12

PRESS HARDER

When you are going through you have to press hard to continue to make it through.

Today you might feel like you want to give up. But look at it like this...when you need to get toothpaste from the tube and it's almost at its end, what do you do? You press...and that's what God needs you to do. Press toward the goal to win the prize! (Philippians 3:14)

Remember, strength does not come from winning. But it is your struggles that develop your strength. When you go through hardships and decide not to surrender, that is strength!

For our light and temporary affliction is producing for us an eternal glory that far outweighs our troubles. (2 Corinthians 4:17)

At the end of the day:

_____
_____
_____
_____
_____
_____
_____
_____
_____
_____
_____
_____
_____

JUNE 13

PRAYERS & PATIENCE = BLESSINGS

It's easy to want to throw in the towel and give up when you feel like your prayers aren't being answered. But are you patiently waiting for The Lord to move or are you trusting your own timing?

Today not only must you pray without ceasing, but you must patiently wait for The Lord to fulfill His promises that He has for your life. (2 Peter 3:9) If He said it, He will do it!! (Numbers 23:19) God's blessings go far beyond anything we could ever dream. But you have to have patience!!

Remember, you must trust God's timing, rely on His promises, wait for His answers, believe in His miracles, and rejoice in His goodness!

At the end of the day:

_____
_____
_____
_____
_____
_____
_____
_____
_____
_____
_____
_____

JUNE 14

PRAYER WILL CHANGE YOUR SITUATION

There is nothing that you are going through today that is too hard for God to get you out of. He says that if you remain in Him and His words remain in you, you may ask for anything you want, and it will be granted unto you! (John 15:7)

Today, God wants you to know that whatever you ask in prayer, believe that you have received it, and it will be yours. (Mark 11:24) Right now start to pray without ceasing (1 Thessalonians 5:17) and God will give you the desires of your heart! (Psalm 37:4)

But when you pray, go into your room and shut the door and pray to your Father who is in secret. And your Father who sees you in secret will reward you. (Matthew 6:6)

At the end of the day:

_____
_____
_____
_____
_____
_____
_____
_____
_____
_____
_____
_____
_____

JUNE 15

PRAY FOR THEM

There might be people in your life that want to see you down and out. Your failure gives them joy.

Today don't worry about "them" because you can't change who they are, but you can pray for them instead.

Remember, bless those who curse you and pray for those who mistreat, hurt and despitefully use you! (Luke 6:28)

But I say to you, Love your enemies and pray for those who persecute you, (Matthew 5:44)

At the end of the day:

_____
_____
_____
_____
_____
_____
_____
_____
_____
_____
_____
_____
_____

JUNE 16

PRAY FOR OTHERS THAN YOURSELF

I want to encourage all of you to try to pray for someone else instead of yourself when you are praying this week. I'm not saying when you pray every day but whether it is tonight, in the morning or tomorrow... but one day this week just take time out of your schedule and pray for a family member, a friend, coworker or a stranger. It will bless you more ways than you think.

A lot of us say that we are Christians and this and that, but we won't even take the time to pray or help someone in need. There should be POWER in YOUR life because you are a Christian.

(Things to make you go hmmm)

And the Lord restored the fortunes of Job, when he had prayed for his friends. And the Lord gave Job twice as much as he had before. (Job 42:10)

At the end of the day:

_____
_____
_____
_____
_____
_____
_____
_____
_____
_____
_____

JUNE 17

PRAISE UNTIL HE LETS GO

The enemy tries to hold on to you and get in your head so that he can confuse you. Once he's in you start to believe the lies he spills. But thank God, we know the devil is actually a LIE!!!

Today it's time to praise in the midst of the adversity and hell that's been clinging on to you for dear life. Release and let it go and only hold on to God's unchanging hand!

Remember, you have to learn how not to let go of your praise until the enemy lets go of you....and even then, you must keep praising on!! (Tera Carissa)

You have established strength Because of Your adversaries, To make the enemy and the revengeful cease." (Psalm 8:2)

But let all those rejoice who put their trust in You; Let them ever shout for joy, because You defend them; Let those also who love Your name Be joyful in You. For You, O Lord, will bless the righteous; with favor You will surround him as with a shield. (Psalm 5:11-12)

At the end of the day:

_____
_____
_____
_____
_____
_____
_____
_____

JUNE 18

PRAISE THROUGH THE PRESSURE

Sometimes when you don't know what to do...the best thing to do is just praise.

I know it seems like things are overwhelming to you and your heart is heavy. But not even the devil in hell, can stop you from praising God.

Remember, if you want to see a real breakthrough from the pressure you are in, learn to get your praise on. Because if God can turn night into day He can turn a burden into a blessing!

Through him then let us continually offer up a sacrifice of praise to God, that is, the fruit of lips that acknowledge his name. (Hebrews 13:15)

At the end of the day:

_____
_____
_____
_____
_____
_____
_____
_____
_____
_____
_____

JUNE 19

PRAISE IN PAIN

Life is hard...and a lot of times life is going to deal you a bad hand. Unfortunately, you have to play the cards you are dealt with. The good news is God will help you play those cards you get.

Today even with all the tears you have cried. The pain you feel and the heartache you have.... you still have enough sense to give Him praise.

Just remember, the deepest level of worship is praising God in spite of pain, thanking God during a trial, trusting Him when tempted, surrendering while suffering and loving Him when He seems distant. (Rick Warren)

Give thanks to the LORD, for he is good! His faithful love endures forever. (Psalm 118:1)

At the end of the day:

JUNE 20

PEACE BE STILL

Don't become frantic when your life seems so overwhelming that you can't even breathe and you say, "Lord now what?" We all have been there, but always remember that one time

Jesus was with His disciples in a boat out on the water when they came upon a horrific storm. The disciples, just like you, were very afraid; but Jesus on the other hand, was asleep and didn't have a clue what was taking place. When the disciples woke Him up to see if He could help, Jesus got up and simply spoke to the storm, "Peace, Be still." And the seas were calm.

Today, know that God has given you His authority to declare peace over your life, your home, your mind, over your family and your circumstances that you will encounter in this life.

Then He arose and rebuked the wind, and said to the sea, "Peace, be still!" And the wind ceased and there was a great calm. (Mark 4:39)

At the end of the day:

_____
_____
_____
_____
_____
_____
_____
_____
_____
_____

JUNE 21

OVERCOMING

Just because you are still going through, God says that you have already overcome. It's time to stop tripping, crying and fighting over something that God has already called you victorious in. (1 Corinthians 15:57)

Today know that the enemy is a lie and he can go back where he came from...because YOU are a winner!

Remember, challenges are what make life interesting, and overcoming them is what makes life meaningful. (Joshua J. Marine)

So, the greater the obstacle, the more joy in overcoming it! (Moliere)

You are from God, little children, and have overcome them; because greater is He who is in you than he who is in the world. (1 John 4:4)

At the end of the day:

_____
_____
_____
_____
_____
_____
_____
_____
_____
_____

JUNE 22

OPPONENT = VICTORY

No one wants to deal with a nasty wicked opponent. But at some point, in your life, you have to face your "Goliath" (1 Samuel 17)

Today you need to recognize that-YES you are going to have to get in the ring. But you won't be in the ring by yourself. This is the time God is elevating you….and in order for you to be elevated you have to face "it" so you can reign!

Remember, you're not going to have victory until you first go head to head with your opponent!

They are-panic-stricken- [but] there was no reason to panic, because God has scattered the bones of those who set up camp against you." (Psalm 53:5)

But you give us victory over our enemies, you put our adversaries to shame. (Psalm 44:7)

At the end of the day:

_____
_____
_____
_____
_____
_____
_____
_____

JUNE 23

ONE DAY THIS WILL BE YOUR TESTIMONY

You may not understand why you are going through what you are going through now, but one day you are going to look back and it will all make sense. Just continue to trust in The Lord with all your heart and lean not on your own understanding; but seek His will and He will show you what to do. (Proverbs 3: 5-6)

Today, thank God from protecting you from what you thought you wanted and blessing you from what He knows you need.

Remember, "This will be one day as if it never was!" (Pastor Tyshawn Gardner)

Making your ear attentive to wisdom and inclining your heart to understanding; yes, if you call out for insight and raise your voice for understanding, if you seek it like silver and search for it as for hidden treasures, then you will understand the fear of the Lord and find the knowledge of God. (Proverbs 2:2-5)

At the end of the day:

_____
_____
_____
_____
_____
_____
_____
_____
_____

JUNE 24

OKAY...IT HAPPENED

No matter how good you are and how many times you do the right thing; at the end of the day sometimes life still isn't fair!

Today, stop focusing on the bad breaks, how someone hurt you and how it wasn't fair. It happened, it's over so it's time to move on.

Remember, forget what's gone, appreciate what still remains and look forward to what's coming next!

I focus on this one thing: Forgetting the past and looking forward to what lies ahead, (Philippians 3:13)

At the end of the day:
_____
_____
_____
_____
_____
_____
_____
_____
_____
_____
_____
_____
_____
_____

JUNE 25

OBEY AND JUST DO IT

When you're obeying God and His Word, your dreams start to come to pass. The problem that was about to take you out becomes null and void! More miracles and abundant blessings will come as soon as you learn to do what you are supposed to do.

Today, I encourage everyone to walk boldly in obedience. Once you do...you will see God's Power and Favor shine all through your life!!!l

Whatever He says to you, do it. (John 2:5)

At the end of the day:

_____
_____
_____
_____
_____
_____
_____
_____
_____
_____
_____
_____
_____
_____

JUNE 26

NOW = GREATER LATER

Yes, it may be a fact that your current "now" doesn't look so great. But if only you had a crystal ball that could show the miracles and wonders that God is going to do for you later. Well NEWSFLASH, He does know; and that is why you must remain steadfast and unmovable. (1 Corinthians 15:58)

Today, make up in your mind that," Yes right now isn't looking good, but I know greater is He that is in me, than He that is in the world. (1 John 4:4) So I'm going to hold on to His unchanging hand. Because there will be a day that I can tell somebody about what my God did for me and how I made it over."

Now give Him your greatest praise in advance, for your biggest comeback yet!

No eye has seen, no ear has heard, and no mind has imagined what God has prepared for those who love him. (1 Corinthians 2:9)

Because Better Days Are Coming!

At the end of the day:
_____
_____
_____
_____
_____
_____
_____
_____
_____

JUNE 27

NOTICE SERVED: EVICTION TO THE ENEMY

The devil doesn't have ownership of anything we possess. The Bible tells us in Psalm 24:1, "The earth is the LORD's, and everything in it," God is the true and rightful owner!!! You can't fret and worry about what the enemy is trying to do and take from you when he doesn't even have ownership of anything.

Today, get your mind right. Take captive of all negative thoughts that have you all bent out of shape and evict Satan out of your mind!

Remember, the devil can't take what belongs to The Father!

"Do not conform to the pattern of this world, but be transformed by the renewing of your mind. Then you will be able to test and approve that God's will is His good.

At the end of the day:

JUNE 28

NOT YOUR WAY...BUT GOD'S

It's hard when you want to step in and take control of things when you think God is taking too long or not even listening to your prayers or cries for help. Fact is He is listening but you are going to have to step back and let God do what He does best...and that is His will and not yours.

Today is the day that you say, "God not my will, but Your will". So even if that means that you have to stand for a little longer, suffer just a tad bit more and be around folks that you know mean you harm...you must do what thus saith the Lord. (Jeremiah5:14)

Remember, after you have suffered a little while....it is the God of all grace that will surely bring you out and restore, strengthen and make you strong and better! (1 Peter 5:10)

Now may the God of peace, who through the blood of the eternal covenant brought back from the dead our Lord Jesus, that great Shepherd of the sheep, equip you with everything good for doing His will, and may He work in us what is pleasing to Him, through Jesus Christ, to whom be glory for ever and ever. Amen. (Hebrews 13:20-21)

At the end of the day:

_____

_____

_____

_____

_____

_____

_____

JUNE 29

NOT TODAY

It's a fact that the enemy comes to kill and destroy. It would be a safe bet to say that we all have someone that is around us, at some point, that every time they get close to you, you have to call out the name JESUS! They make it their passion to try to take you down. But what they don't know is that God is for YOU!

Today, tell the enemy, "Not Today!" Not another day will you have to let Satan try to take you out. The Devil is a lie!!!!!! YOU ARE GOD'S CHILD! God said, "That He is shifting your atmosphere." What the enemy is trying to do to harm you, God is using to make them be your footstool.

The Opposition is Shrinking Today!

The LORD will cause your enemies who rise against you to be defeated before you. They shall come out against you one way and flee before you seven ways." (Deuteronomy 28:7)

At the end of the day:

_____
_____
_____
_____
_____
_____
_____
_____
_____

JUNE 30

NOT THE END, BUT A NEW BEGINNING

God knows what you have been through. Your tears, pain and heartache have not gone unnoticed.

He has kept track of all of your sorrow and collected each tear you have shed in a bottle. (Psalm 56:8)

He has been there through it all. What the enemy meant for evil, God is going to use for your Good.

Today know that God is wiping away every tear from your eye and there will be no more mourning, crying, pain and heartache.

For the former things are in the past and He is giving you a new beginning. (Revelation 21:4)

Remember, you sowed in tears and now you will reap with joy! (Psalm 126:5)

For I am about to do something new. See, I have already begun! Do you not see it? I will make a pathway through the wilderness. I will create rivers in the dry wasteland. (Isaiah 43:19)

At the end of the day:

_____

_____

_____

_____

_____

_____

JULY 1

NOT DESTROYED

There may have been folks in your life that tried every attempt possible to take you out. But by the grace of God you are still standing!

Today, you may have gotten bent all the way back like a palm tree on a sunny, windy day in Florida. But God's hand was never off your life.

Remember, they may have knocked you down, and that's on them. But a week later if you are still down that's on you! (Reverend Al Sharpton)

NOW GET ON UP! You may be hurt, but you are NOT broken and you are NOT destroyed!!!

"We are hunted down, but never abandoned by God. We get knocked down, but we are not destroyed." (2 Corinthians 4:9 NLT)

Persecuted, but not abandoned; struck down, but not destroyed. (2 Corinthians 4:9 NIV)

At the end of the day:

_____
_____
_____
_____
_____
_____
_____
_____

JULY 2

NOBODY SAID THE ROAD WOULD BE EASY

I'm sure you have heard at some point in your life the saying, "Nobody said that the road would be easy, but I know He didn't bring me this far to leave me now." Well fact is that is very true. God says that "He will never leave you nor forsake you." (Hebrews 13:5)

Today, be at ease knowing just as God was with Moses He will be with You. (Joshua 1:5) There is no need to be afraid or discouraged any longer, for God is with you always. He is strengthening you and holding you up with his victorious righteous right hand. He has you!!! (Isaiah 41:10)

Remember, nobody said that the road would be easy, but you know He didn't bring you this far to leave you now. So, you can't give up! Just trust Him!

Be strong and courageous. Do not fear or be in dread of them, for it is the Lord your God who goes with you. He will not leave you or forsake you. (Deuteronomy 31:6)

At the end of the day:

_____
_____
_____
_____
_____
_____
_____
_____

JULY 3

NOBODY GREATER

You might be going through. I mean down on your luck. You muster up the courage to ask for help only to get denied and folks are talking about you.

Today you need to know that with man it can be impossible; but with God, all things are possible. (Matthew 19:26)

Remember, there is nobody greater that can help you through this, but The Lord.

KEEP STANDING!

My Father, who has given them to me, is greater than all; no one can snatch them out of my Father's hand. (John 10:29)

At the end of the day:

_____
_____
_____
_____
_____
_____
_____
_____
_____
_____
_____

JULY 4

NO TIME TO BE WEARY OR WORRIED

Some people think it's easier said than done when you say, "I'm gonna let it go and not worry about it." Fact is you have to let it go and give it to God; for He hasn't given you a spirit of fear. (2 Timothy 1:7) He doesn't want you anxious, weary or worried. (Matthew 6:25-34)

Today is the day that you no longer carry the dead weight on you. It's not the time to give up, but it is the time to get up!!!

So get on up…. because at the right time God will show you mighty works if you hold fast and be unmovable.

Let us not become weary in doing good; for at the proper time, we will reap a harvest if we do not give up. (Galatians 6:9)

At the end of the day:

JULY 5

NO NEED TO BEG

What you are going through now is painful. If you talk about it, it might make you cry. You've asked for help, but there seems to be no one around that can help you. Leaving you feeling helpless.

Today know that you don't have to beg anyone for anything. You belong to God and He has given you everything you need. (1 Corinthians 3:23) & (2 Thessalonians 1:2)

If it's meant for you...ultimately you don't have to beg for it; because you will never have to sacrifice your dignity for your destiny.

Remember, you are luxury and a very special treasure to The Lord. So, consider yourself like a Rolls Royce and Bentley car. Meaning, they don't have commercials on tv for a reason because they know their value.

I have been young, and now am old, yet I have not seen the righteous forsaken or his children begging for bread. (Psalm 37:25)

At the end of the day:

_____
_____
_____
_____
_____
_____
_____
_____
_____

JULY 6

NO NEED TO BE AFRAID

God doesn't want you afraid. For He hasn't given you a spirit of fear... but of power. (2 Timothy 1:7) You can't be afraid of those who threaten you. For the time will come when God will bring every deed into judgment, including everything hidden; whether it is good or evil. (Ecclesiastes12:14)

Today, don't let your hearts be troubled or afraid. (John 14:27) Those thoughts are not from God but from the enemy. For God is not a God of confusion but of peace. (1 Corinthians 14:33)

Remember, God wants you to be strong, courageous and not scared at things coming your way. He is with you in the midst of it all!!! (Joshua 1:9)

Do not be afraid of them," the LORD said to Joshua, "for I have given you victory over them. Not a single one of them will be able to stand up to you. (Joshua 10:8)

At the end of the day:

_____
_____
_____
_____
_____
_____
_____
_____
_____

JULY 7

NO EVIL FOR EVIL

Sometimes it can be hard to sit and stand while your enemy attacks and comes from you. But God has said, "vengeance is His and He will repay." (Romans 12:19)

Today, don't let what people are doing or saying drive you to take matters into your own hands. In due time their feet will slip, and their day of disaster will come. (Deuteronomy 32:35) All you have to do is be still and stand!

Remember, do not repay evil for evil, but continue to wait for the Lord and he will avenge you! (Romans 12:17) (Proverbs20:22)

Don't repay evil for evil. Don't retaliate with insults when people insult you. Instead, pay them back with a blessing. That is what God has called you to do, and He will bless you for it. (1 Peter 3:9)

At the end of the day:

JULY 8

NEVER STOP PRAYING

As you go through life, some days will be hard. You will have days where you might find it hard to pray. That is when you know you need to pray the most.

Today, if you are heartbroken and your eyes are filled with tears, dig deep down inside and cry out to God and tell him what is on your heart. He is listening.

Remember, life isn't fair but it is life. And it is worth fighting for!

Is anyone among you suffering? Let him pray. (James 5:13)

At the end of the day:

JULY 9

NEVER AGAIN

God tells us that if we humble ourselves unto Him, He will lift us up. (James 4:10) So if you know this....it's time to get humble and recognize where your help comes from.

Today tell the devil, NEVER AGAIN!

> Never again will you be suicidal!
> Never again will you be defeated!
> Never again will you be depressed!
> Never again will you be stuck!
> Never again will you rob Peter to pay Paul.
> Never again will you go backwards!
> Never again will you lose your power!
> NEVER!

Remember, the Spirit of God that raised Jesus from the dead lives in YOU! (Romans 8:11)

Therefore, there is now no condemnation for those who are in Christ Jesus,

At the end of the day:

_____
_____
_____
_____
_____
_____
_____
_____

JULY 10

MOVING ON

Moving forward is often painful, but very necessary. It is far better than giving up and sliding backwards. God is doing a good work in you and He is getting ready to do even bigger and better things for and in you. None of these things will happen if you will continue to hold on to people, places or circumstances that are holding you down.

Today, ask God to fill you with holy determination so you can continue to move forward and go in the right direction.

Remember, There is Power and Purpose in Closed Doors!

I will instruct you and teach you in the way you should go; I will counsel you with my eye upon you. (Psalm 32:8)

At the end of the day:

_____
_____
_____
_____
_____
_____
_____
_____
_____
_____
_____
_____
_____

JULY 11

MOVE OUT OF THE WAY

A lot of times you sit and pray and ask God to work and move in your life, but you are trying to handle things on your own. In actuality, you are blocking God from doing what He needs to do. Sometimes you need to move and be quiet and let God do his good work on your behalf.

Today, be quiet, be still and get out of God's way and let Him move on your behalf. He heard your cries and prayers. So, let Him go to work. Turn it over to Him and leave it there. Quit taking it back.

Remember, if you want God to fix it...well then MOVE! Let Him get to work. He has this!

Many are the plans in the mind of a man, but it is the purpose of the Lord that will stand. (Proverbs 19:21)

At the end of the day:

___
___
___
___
___
___
___
___
___
___
___
___

JULY 12

MORE PROBLEMS BUT LOUDER PRAISES

With my mouth I will give great thanks to the LORD; I will praise him in the midst of the throng (Psalm 109:30)

Many of you, I know, are going through some trying times right now. It is established that the devil is busy and his main goal is to kill and destroy families. He might think that he has you backed in a corner because he is coming at you every which way possible. However, this is the time to get your praise on and open up your mouth and give God your biggest, "Thank You's" and Praises like you have never done before!

It's quite simple, the enemy wants to shut you up and keep your mouth closed. But he is a lie! No weapon formed against you shall prosper! God is the ONLY one that will take your sorrow and turn it into joy. The anguish and despair you have, He will give you hope for tomorrow.

Let's face it...there are things in this life that we are facing that are impossible to fix. But you have the most powerful weapon with you at all times and that is your praise and worship to Him. I know the situation isn't nowhere near to being fixed. (So you think) But have you truly opened up your mouth and given Him praise in the midst of the storm?

This week, show God what you are really working with. Every time you are about to get hit right in the face and you know it's satan, begin to open up your mouth and tell Him, "Thank You". Give praises now and rebuke the enemy up off ya!

Praise the LORD! Give thanks to the LORD, for He is good! His faithful love endures forever. (Psalm 106:1)

At the end of the day:

JULY 13

MAKE GOD FAMOUS

Are you telling others about the goodness of the Father? Everybody doesn't know Him. Put Him on blast! Because you won't talk about Him and afraid of what others will say about you... you will never experience a true intimate relationship with God.

Today, don't allow the things of this world to keep you from experiencing God's presence. Start right now by spending quality and one on one time with Him. Humble yourself to the Father and realize without Him there would be no YOU!

I am the vine; you are the branches. If you remain in me and I in you, you will bear much fruit; apart from Me you can do nothing. (John 15:5)

At the end of the day:

JULY 14

LOSE TO WIN

In this life, we live, sometimes you have to let go and lose some things to win again.

Today, hold your head up. You may have lost your job, house, furniture and car. But praise Him for the air mattress, bus pass and the money you still got in your pocket.

Remember, God will restore to you what the enemy tried to steal. Just keep on praising the name of The Lord and you will have plenty and be satisfied! (Joel 2:26)

Instead of your shame there shall be a double portion; instead of dishonor they shall rejoice in their lot; therefore, in their land they shall possess a double portion; they shall have everlasting joy. (Isaiah 61:7)

At the end of the day:

_____
_____
_____
_____
_____
_____
_____
_____
_____
_____
_____

JULY 15

LORD, HELP ME

"Fear not, for I am with you; be not dismayed, for I am your God; I will strengthen you, I will help you, I will uphold you with my righteous right hand." (Isaiah 41:10)

I have always been told that I am extremely hard on myself. I know that I am my own worst critic. It is easy for me to receive an email or a phone call from someone going through and reciting a scripture or telling them they know already the outcome because they know God. However, at the same time, I'm wise enough to know that I need to practice what I preach.

"The LORD answered me and set me in a large place. The LORD is for me; I will not fear; what can man do to me? The LORD is for me among those who help me...It is better to take refuge in the LORD than to trust in man." (Psalms 118)

The psalmist had every reason to be afraid. Surrounded by all those enemies, it was overwhelming. He could have felt that was it, this fight is over before it even begins. But he cried to the Lord and took refuge in Him. Then his attitude completely changed. He realized he did not have to fear any person or organization as long as he trusted in God. The Lord answered him by setting him free.

A lot of you today may be feeling just like the psalmist, overwhelmed and defeated. Ultimately you may feel that you are surrounded on every side, completely vulnerable, outnumbered, and unsure of what to do about your situation. I just want to tell you that God wants you to cry out to Him, take refuge in Him, and believe His promises, declaring them to be true in your life. Then He promises that you will have freedom from all fear that is holding you captive.

At the end of the day:

JULY 16

LOOK TO GOD

"Looking to Jesus, the founder and perfecter of our faith," (Hebrews 12:2)

We are all going to have a bad day, a bad week and some even a bad month every now and then. But you have to be glad that God tells us that, "it's temporary."

I'm not sure who this is for, but if you are like me and you keep trying and trying and trying and feel like you just can't catch a break…well I just say, "though He slay me, yet will I trust Him" (Job 13:15)

Today, this week and here on out I pray that all of you (including me) will look to God. The Bible says that Jesus is the Author and Finisher of our Faith. TRUST God He knows what He is doing!

I DECLARE & DECREE A BREAKTHROUGH IS COMING!

At the end of the day:

_____
_____
_____
_____
_____
_____
_____
_____
_____
_____

JULY 17

LITTLE OR GREAT FAITH?

If I was to ask all of you do you have Faith? The majority of you would say yes. My next question would be, "is it little or great?" Anyone can say that they have faith, but when it is time to test and activate it, it's a whole other story.

When you have little faith, you will believe a lie from the enemy before the Word of God. When you have great faith, there is no limit to what God will do for you.

Today, activate the GREAT FAITH inside of you. Let God take you higher than any human can. When you believe in God's Word and start to literally live it. Then put it into action and watch God remove mountains that haven't even come across your path yet.

So that your faith might not rest in the wisdom of men, but in the power of God. (1 Corinthians 2:5)

At the end of the day:

JULY 18

LET YOUR LIGHT SHINE

You are God's Child and there is nothing in this world that you can't do if you put your mind to it. The enemy may have tried to detour and discourage you, making your past mistakes define you. Just know that with God on your side there is nothing that you can't achieve or accomplish in this world if you just believe.

Today walk by faith and not by sight. (2 Corinthians 5:7) In the natural it may look impossible, but know that you can do all things in Christ whom gives you strength. (Philippians 4:13)

Remember, those who are wise will shine as bright as the sky, and those who lead many to righteousness will shine like the stars forever. (Daniel 12:3)

The path of the righteous is like the morning sun, shining ever brighter till the full light of day. (Proverbs 4:18)

At the end of the day:

_____
_____
_____
_____
_____
_____
_____
_____
_____
_____
_____

JULY 19

LET YOUR ENEMIES PUSH YOU

Don't fret, worry or even trip when your haters and enemies try to attack you. (Isaiah 41:10) Began immediately to praise and thank the Father that greater is coming your way.

Today recognize that when you are getting attacked that God has a blessing for you, that the devil doesn't want you to have.

Remember, you can't avoid it if you are getting ready to be delivered from evil.

I will pour out a blessing so great you won't have enough room to take it in! Try it! Put me to the test! (Malachi 3:10)

At the end of the day:

JULY 20

LET THEM WALK

In life people are going to come and go in your life. There is no need to be sad or down about their choice to leave. Let them walk on out!

Today, hold your head up high, even if your spouse, friend or family member decided to walk away from you. Just know that God has promised to never leave nor forsake you. (Deuteronomy 31:6)

Remember, when people walk away from your life you must let them walk. Your destiny is never tied to anybody who has left.

Stay Prayed Up & Encouraged ~

But do not be afraid of them; remember well what the LORD your God did to Pharaoh and to all Egypt. (Deuteronomy 7:18)

At the end of the day:

_____
_____
_____
_____
_____
_____
_____
_____
_____
_____
_____

JULY 21

LET THEM COME

You may feel as if everywhere you turn, the enemy is coming for you. On your job, in your marriage, at home and sometimes even at church. Well that's his job, he plays mind games because ultimately, he comes to kill and destroy. (John 10:10)

Today, tell the enemy, "come on and take your best shot!" See, here is the thing.... you have a treasure and he wants it. But more importantly, you have to know that YOU ARE A TREASURE! And God has a hedge fence of protection around you. (Job 1:10)

So he can come for you, and he can come all day long; but you are not alone. God is right there shielding, protecting, covering and blocking the enemy's evil tricks and schemes. Remember, a thousand may fall at your side, ten thousand at your right hand, but it will not come near you. (Psalm 91:7)

At the end of the day:

_____
_____
_____
_____
_____
_____
_____
_____
_____

JULY 22

HATERS CAN'T TAKE NOTHING FROM YOU

Haters are going to hate. It doesn't matter what you do. If you blessed the world with cars, they would still complain and say, "Why didn't you give free gas with it?" It will always be something.

Fact is you still must pray for those who mistreat and talk about you. (Luke 6:28) Yes, it isn't easy. But you still must do it.

Remember, what God has ordained for your life can't no hater take it away.

Focus on God's Love not people's hate. (Trent Shelton)

At the end of the day:

JULY 23

LET IT TRAIN YOU

In this path called life that we are on. There are going to be setups and setbacks. It can cause us to feel, at times, that we have failed and nothing seems to be working out in our favor. But we know that the devil is a lie!

Today, let all the bad breaks, obstacles, difficulties and even setbacks train you to focus on the eye of the prize. Don't let the failures define and stop you...but let them train you to make you better.

It's time to learn from them!

Remember, what you went through in the past does not dictate your present. (Joyce Meyer)

For whatever was written in former days was written for our instruction, that through endurance and through the encouragement of the Scriptures, we might have hope. (Romans 15:4)

At the end of the day:

_____
_____
_____
_____
_____
_____
_____
_____

JULY 24

LET GOD WORK IN YOUR LIFE

It's one thing to know God, but it's another to really have a relationship with Him. When you are down and out and folks have turned they back on you; you can stand tall because you already know, though you walk through the valley of the shadow of death you will fear no evil... because your Savior goes with you. (Psalm 23:4)

Today, turn it over to God and let Him work in your life. I know you don't understand. But just trust in the Lord with all your heart, and do not lean on your own understanding. (Proverbs 3:5)

Remember, even when you can't see it, know that He is working everything out for your good!!

And those who know your name put their trust in You, for You, O Lord, have not forsaken those who seek You. (Psalm 9:10)

At the end of the day:

_____
_____
_____
_____
_____
_____
_____
_____
_____
_____

JULY 25

LET GOD TAKE CARE OF THEM

Your enemy might be sitting pretty high right now; at least so they think. They might have the position, power, money and authority, but you have God on your side.

Today, hold your head up and don't shed not one tear. The God of Peace will soon crush satan under your feet. There is nothing for you to fear. You have the grace of The Lord with you and you are going to be just fine. Jesus is with you! (Romans 16:20)

When these things begin to take place, stand up and lift up your heads, because your redemption is drawing near. (Luke 21:28)

At the end of the day:

JULY 26

LET GOD SEE YOUR FAITH

God is not attracted to our problems, but He is attracted to our praise. God wants all of us to exercise our Faith. As soon as you start doing your part and God sees it, extraordinary things will begin to happen. Faith opens the door for God to move. So today and every day activate your faith and watch the hand of God move in every area of your life!

And when he saw their faith... (Luke 5:20)

At the end of the day:

JULY 27

LET GOD PAY BACK

God is just: He will pay back trouble to those who trouble you. (2 Thessalonians 1:6)

It's human nature to get caught up and want to do tit for tat when someone hurts you. But I've come to learn that God TRULY & WILL take care of the ones that have hurt you, better than we could ever do.

Recently, two girlfriends had told me a story about Sheryl Underwood. She is a co-host for "The Talk" on CBS. It was a powerful life learned lesson she had experience with three other women from "The Queens of Comedy Tour". It was a touching story because she overheard the ladies on a conference call talking about her very badly and she was on mute. She never unmuted her line, she just listened and took notes. When watching the interview this morning she said she was, "bruised, but not broken". Take the lesson and apply it to your everyday life.

Pray, Stand, and Don't Let The Enemy See You Sweat! Silence Sometimes is Better Said Than Anything!

Remember, Sheryl Underwood's statement, "I Was Bruised, But Not Broken.

At the end of the day:

JULY 28

LET GOD DO IT

When you try to do things on your own, sometimes you will end up more hurt than ever. Crying like never before. Chaos and destruction can come from you just saying, "I can do this, fix it and work it out all by myself."

Today, if you really want to see a change, just let God do it. You have seen how things turn out when you handle it...so turn it over to the one and only and let Him work it out for your good!

Remember, can't nobody do you like Jesus...so give it to Him. He won't let you down!

Will it be easy? No! But will it be worth it? ABSOLUTELY!

At the end of the day:

___
___
___
___
___
___
___
___
___
___
___
___
___
___

JULY 29

LET GOD DEAL WITH THE OUTCOME

You can't control something that you are going through or even dealing with when you have asked God to fix it.

Today stop worrying about the things that are out of your control. When you say, you are giving it over to The Lord; you must do just that and let Him work it out.

Remember, if you are worrying about it, there is no need to pray... and if you are praying about it, there is no need to worry. (Think about it)

Stay Prayed Up & Encouraged!!!

Now to him who is able to do far more abundantly than all that we ask or think, according to the power at work within us. (Ephesians 3:20)

At the end of the day:

_____
_____
_____
_____
_____
_____
_____
_____
_____
_____

JULY 30

LEAN NOT UNTO THY OWN UNDERSTANDING

"Trust in the Lord with all your heart, and do not lean on your own understanding. In all your ways acknowledge him, and he will make straight your paths." (Proverbs 3:5-6)

In the Bible in Proverbs and Psalms you can see where our actions and attitude can result in God's Favor, but we must have understanding.

Some of you are new to receive my messages but I know I sound like a broken record to some when I say put your spiritual armor on every day because the devil walks around like a roaring lion to see whom he can devour. You can wake up in a good mood on your merry way and *Boom* get hit with something from left field that can throw your day off course. But if you are handcuffed with the Father NOTHING can un-move you.

Good understanding produces favor, but the way of the treacherous is hard. (Proverbs 13:15)

I can't stress enough why it is so important to seek wisdom and understanding. You have to realize the importance of seeking God and knowing His Word and more importantly...putting it into practice of your everyday life and routine. Psalms 111:10 says, "The fear of the Lord is the beginning of wisdom; all those who practice it have a good understanding. His praise endures forever!"

When you start to praise and honor God and put His commandments into practice, that leads to the Scripture of Proverbs 16:22 that's says, "Understanding is a well-spring of life unto him that hath it; But the correction of fools is their folly."

I pray that all of you seek His Wisdom and Understanding. Study His Word Daily, and put it into practice. Fear God, and submit your life to Him.

At the end of the day:

JULY 31

KNOW WHO IS IN CONTROL

If you are in a situation and you feel alone, it's time that you know that with God, you are never alone! So stop sitting there trying to take matters in your own hands and trust God! God is amazing, and his grace is sufficient enough to give you everything that you need.

Today, while it might look a little gloomy and dim. The truth is you have the Creator of this amazing universe on your side! He knows all things and has made all things. There is no need to worry because you're his child...and He is always protecting YOU!

I have said these things to you, that in me you may have peace. In the world you will have tribulation. But take heart; I have overcome the world. John 16:33

At the end of the day:

AUGUST 1

KNOW WHERE YOUR HELP COMES FROM

My help comes from the LORD, who made heaven and earth. (Psalm 121:2)

I know a lot of you are going through and some days it seems you don't know what to do. It can be completely overwhelming. Recently, actor/comedian Robin Williams committing suicide has drawn so much needed attention on depression, that is truly long overdue.

I was contacted this week by a friend that was clearly suicidal. I know because I've been that low before. The one thing she asked me before I gave her the number to get help was, What got me through it? My response....God.

Today, I want all of us to have a Job like Faith. We all should know who Job was in the Bible. He had everything taken from him and He would not curse God... no matter what.

My question is...Who are you? If things are good, do you still praise Him? Go to church? Read your word or do you just go to Him when you need Him for something?

He is Not a Sometimes God. So don't go to Him Just Sometimes. If You Do, You Will Get Sometimes Results!

At the end of the day:
_____
_____
_____
_____
_____

AUGUST 2

KNOCK KNOCK

When trouble comes knocking at your door, you don't have to be afraid. God is with and for you. He is not the one who is against you, so don't turn away from Him now! You must keep your eyes on Him and trust that He has a plan. Somehow and someway He is going to make that crooked place straight and your rough place smooth.

Today, lift your eyes only to Jesus because He IS the Author and Finisher of your Faith… and a very present help in the day of trouble.

Looking unto Jesus the author and finisher of our faith; (Hebrews12:2)

At the end of the day:

_____
_____
_____
_____
_____
_____
_____
_____
_____
_____
_____
_____

AUGUST 3

KNEEL

I know things have been hard lately. You don't know what you are going to do or what is going to happen with you or your situation. Although I don't need to know what every single person is going through. I do know that no matter what it is, all you have to do is kneel and turn it over to The Lord in prayer.

Today, as you go about your day and you are feeling a bit down and troubled. Get on bended knees and pray like you have never prayed before and ask God to fix it. No matter what it is, just tell him that you want HIM to intervene and fix it.

If you really want to see a change in your life; start by staying on your knees in prayer and watch what will happen!

Hear me when I call, O God of my righteousness: you have enlarged me when I was in distress; have mercy on me, and hear my prayer. (Psalms 4:1)

At the end of the day:

_____
_____
_____
_____
_____
_____
_____
_____
_____
_____

AUGUST 4

KEEP SMILING

I know there is a lot going on right now in your life. 100 problems... but guess what? God has a million blessings to give you through it all.

Today, don't be down and discouraged. Put a smile on your face and keep on walking into your blessings. Whether you think so or not, but God is seeing all the turmoil you are going through and every tear you have shed. Trust, it is not in vain.

Remember, They that sow in tears shall reap in joy. (Psalm 126:5)

At the end of the day:

AUGUST 5

KEEP PUSHING

Sometimes it feels the more you pray the worse your situation can get. But someone needs to know today that God hasn't forgotten about you at all. I know you want to throw in the towel and say, "just forget it, I give up." But the devil is a lie. You are going to keep moving and push your way on through.

Today, realize that the enemy wants you to give up. But you have to declare and decree that nothing is going to stop you now. You can't and you won't stop!!!

Get up, take up your bed, and walk. (John 5:8)

At the end of the day:

AUGUST 6

KEEP PRAYING PERSISTENTLY

When you need something it's easy to pray and call out to God. But oftentimes when you've been praying, it seems as if God isn't answering your prayers.

Today, don't quit because your prayer hasn't been answered yet. Instead be persistent in prayer.

Remember, the value of persistent prayer is not that He will hear us, but that we will finally hear Him!

Pray in the Spirit at all times and on every occasion. Stay alert and be persistent in your prayers for all believers everywhere. (Ephesians 6:18)

At the end of the day:

_____
_____
_____
_____
_____
_____
_____
_____
_____
_____
_____
_____

AUGUST 7

KEEP PRAYING & STOP WORRYING

There is nothing that you are going through that you can't take to God and talk to Him about.

Today, I know that you are having a difficult time and you think that no one understands, but you can rest assure that before you were even born that God knew you when you were in your mother's womb; (Jeremiah 1:5) and He knew that this trouble and storm was coming your way. So just trust Him, and if He brought it your way, He will see you through it.

Remember, trouble doesn't last always. So, keep praying and stop worrying!

Never worry about anything. Instead, in every situation, let your petitions be made known to God through prayers and requests, with thanksgiving. (Philippians 4:6)

At the end of the day:

_____
_____
_____
_____
_____
_____
_____
_____
_____

AUGUST 8

KEEP ON TICKING

The enemy wants to see you sweat! Truth be told they are really intimidated by you. They keep on trying to push and knock you down. But you have made up in your mind that. "I can take a lick and keep on ticking!!!"

Today, you must know that God hasn't given you a spirit of fear but of power and a sound mind!

(1 Timothy 2:7) There is no need to do tit for tat…Let God handle it. The battle is not yours to fight. That is why you are able to roll with the punches and take the hits that they keep on throwing at you.

Remember; give no opportunity to the devil and (Ephesians 4:27) don't let it affect or faze you. God says, "That He will defend and avenge for you; while moving you forward!" (Jeremiah 51:36) "For the Lord, will take up their case and will exact life for life. (Proverbs 22:23)

At the end of the day:

_____
_____
_____
_____
_____
_____
_____
_____
_____

AUGUST 9

KEEP ON PRAISING

When life starts to take a toll, one of the first things that we all do is complain about it. I get it; you are frustrated so why not discuss it and vent about what is going on. The problem is God doesn't want to hear our moans and groans. He wants us to open up our mouth and get our praise on. He wants to know that no matter what it is looking like we still trust Him.

Today, if you are in some horrible situations in your life and you truly don't see a way out. Open up your mouth and tell God Thank You. Tell Him Thank You that you are still breathing and even though you can't see it you trust Him and Him only to make a way when there seems like there is no way. Speak from your heart and let the praise of thanksgiving leap from your mouth to Heaven. God will surely hear your cries, your praises and He will knock down every obstacle that is hindering and blocking you from moving forward.

So, Praise Him, Thank Him and Worship Him if you really want to see a change in your circumstances.

The LORD is my strength and my defense; he has become my salvation. He is my God, and I will praise Him, my father's God, and I will exalt Him. (Exodus 15:2)

At the end of the day:

_____
_____
_____
_____
_____

AUGUST 10

KEEP ON KEEPING ON

God never said that the road would be easy but He has promised that He would never leave nor forsake us. (Deuteronomy 31:6)

Today as bad as you feel and hurtful as it has been, God needs you to keep on keeping on. You must keep pressing toward the mark for the prize in Christ Jesus. (Philippians 3:14)

Remember, success is not final. Failure is not fatal, but it is the courage to continue that counts! (Winston Churchill)

It was good for me to be afflicted so that I might learn your decrees. (Psalm 119:71)

At the end of the day:

_____
_____
_____
_____
_____
_____
_____
_____
_____
_____
_____
_____
_____
_____

AUGUST 11

KEEP LOOKING TO GOD

Life can be a trip! People can turn their backs on you and then turn on you without even blinking an eye. Don't fall victims to the devil's wicked and evil schemes.

Today don't get caught up worrying about the enemy and what he is up too. Instead keep your eyes fixed on Jesus and He will take care of you. (Hebrews 12:2)

Remember, the enemy is going to try to throw you off your game, but keep your eyes unto the hills, from which your help comes from! (Psalm 121:1)

Lift up your eyes on high and see who has created these stars. The One who leads forth their host by number, He calls them all by name. Because of the greatness of His might and the strength of His power, Not one of them is missing. (Isaiah 40:26)

At the end of the day:

AUGUST 12

KEEP IT MOVING

God wants you to be victorious. He doesn't want anything to stop you from the promises that He has for your life! You must trust Him and know that His plans are to prosper you and not to harm you. (Jeremiah 29:11)

Today, I want you to keep it moving. Don't let anyone steal your joy. The enemy is only attacking you because he sees what God is about to do to you and for your life. But you won't receive it if you are caught up in the past.

So, keep it moving and get ready to receive abundant blessings from above.

Not that I have already obtained this or am already perfect, but I press on to make it my own, because Christ Jesus has made me His own. Brothers, I do not consider that I have made it my own. But one thing I do: forgetting what lies behind and straining forward to what lies ahead, I press on toward the goal for the prize of the upward call of God in Christ Jesus. (Philippians 3:12-14)

At the end of the day:

_____
_____
_____
_____
_____
_____
_____

AUGUST 13

KEEP DOING YOUR PART

It can be hard doing the right thing when it looks as if the enemy is winning. You can't let your mind play tricks on you. The devil knows what he is doing, which is why you have to put on the full armor of God, so that you can take your stand against the devil's schemes. (Ephesians 6:11)

Today continue to stand, press, pray and let The Lord fight your battles. You are a child of the Most High God. There is nothing that the enemy can do to you because The Lord is protecting and keeping you from all harm and evil that is trying to touch you. (Psalm 121:7)

Keep doing your part and watch God keep you under His everlasting arms for refuge. He is driving out the enemy on your behalf and saying, "DESTROY THEM" (Deuteronomy 33:27)

Don't be afraid. Just stand still and watch the LORD rescue you today. (Exodus 14:13)

At the end of the day:

_____
_____
_____
_____
_____
_____
_____
_____

AUGUST 14

JUST SAY, JESUS!

There are days that sometimes you can't say anything at all. Because if you do...you might curse or begin to cry. So you keep quiet. But that's Satan! Don't fall for his schemes!

Today start calling out and saying "JESUS!" Don't complain don't say anything. Open up your mouth and just say, "JESUS". He has the authority to break every chain and to change every situation that you are going through. No matter how big and how hopeless it looks, God is bigger.

Remember, there is POWER in the name of JESUS!!!

Therefore, God has highly exalted Him and bestowed on Him the name that is above every name, so that at the name of Jesus every knee should bow, in heaven and on earth and under the earth, and every tongue confess that Jesus Christ is Lord, to the glory of God the Father. (Philippians 2:9-11)

At the end of the day:

_____
_____
_____
_____
_____
_____
_____
_____
_____

AUGUST 15

JUDGEMENT FOR: PAIN & SUFFERING

The nights that you have been up pacing the floors and laying on a pillow soaked full of tears hasn't gone unnoticed. God is getting ready to reward you full judgment for your pain and suffering that you've endured.

Today know that it is a cost associated with what you have gone through. God wasn't sitting on the sideline commentating and looking at you fall to pieces. He knew before the disaster hit how it was going to go down. And now He is going to watch you get back up with His full force behind you.

Remember, pain and suffering have come into your life. But pain, sorrow and suffering are kisses from Jesus...and it's a sign that you have come so close to Him that He can kiss you! (Mother Teresa)

And after you have suffered a little while, the God of all grace, who has called you to His eternal glory in Christ, will Himself restore, confirm, strengthen, and establish you. (1 Peter 5:10)

At the end of the day:

_____
_____
_____
_____
_____
_____
_____
_____

AUGUST 16

JESUS MADE A WAY FOR YOU

A lot of people got it twisted!!!! They think that because they call on mamma or daddy, sister or brother and sometimes even a friend or cousin to help them out a time or two, that's how they got out of trouble or who made a way. Well the devil is a lie!!!

Today, you need to recognize truly where your help comes from; The Lord. (Psalm 121:2) God is our refuge and strength, always ready to help in times of trouble. (Psalm 46:1)

Remember, even in your darkest hour and your worst of worst times. He is your shelter and your refuge when you are in trouble and need Him the most ...ONLY Him! (Psalm 9:9)

"O my people, trust in him at all times. Pour out your heart to Him, for God is our refuge. (Psalm 62:8)

At the end of the day:

AUGUST 17

I'VE NEVER

I've never been hurt like this!
I've never cried like this!
I've never been broke like this!
I've never felt pain like this!
I've never been betrayed like this!
I've never been this low!
I've never dealt with anything like this!
I've just NEVER!

Today, God needs YOU need to know, "I've never seen the righteous forsaken nor His seed begging for bread!!!!" (Psalm 37:25)

So, no matter what it looks like...God is still in it and HE WILL take care of YOU!

At the end of the day:

_____
_____
_____
_____
_____
_____
_____
_____

AUGUST 18

IT'S WHAT YOU'RE MADE OF

You really never know what you're made of or how strong you are, until you are faced with a trial and a severe storm in your life.

Today you need to know that you were built to last and not break. God has called you victorious. You are the head and not the tail. Whether you know it or not....you got this!!!!

Remember, God won't give you more than you can bear ...He might let you bend a little bit, but He won't let you break!

No temptation has overtaken you except what is common to mankind. And God is faithful; He will not let you be tempted beyond what you can bear. But when you are tempted, He will also provide a way out so that you can endure it. (1 Corinthians 10:13)

At the end of the day:

_____
_____
_____
_____
_____
_____
_____
_____
_____
_____
_____

AUGUST 19

IT'S UNDER YOUR FEET

You are probably feeling like you are a Heavyweight Boxing Champion of The World the way you have been ducking and diving from the enemy's swings and punches here lately. I mean he has been coming full force. Being very destructive and devastating to your life. But God says hold tight, "I'll make your enemies your footstool." (Luke 20:43)

Today, you have to know that God has already stored up the punishment for the wicked. Let Him repay! (Job 21:19) It's imperative to know that God remembers and knows good and evil deeds. He will give back as given; paying double for what was done. (Revelation 18:5-6)

Remember, it is the God of peace who will soon crush satan under your feet. (Romans 16:20)

The Lord said to my Lord: "Sit at my right hand until I put your enemies under your feet. (Matthew 22:44)

At the end of the day:

_____
_____
_____
_____
_____
_____
_____
_____

AUGUST 20

IT'S TIME TO PRAY

Life is hard but it is worth living for. You can't throw in the towel because you have been thrown some bad blows. Never underestimate the power of prayer. It's time to pray your way out of the storm!

Today stop worrying about this and that and pray about everything.

Remember, when it gets too hard to stand and continue on; just kneel and pray.

Do not be anxious about anything, but in everything by prayer and supplication with thanksgiving, let your requests be made known to God. (Philippians 4:6)

At the end of the day:

_____
_____
_____
_____
_____
_____
_____
_____
_____
_____
_____
_____

AUGUST 21

IT'S REVEALING

All the pain and hurt that you have been dealing with lately does have a purpose. It may seem like you are going to die where you're at. But thank God, we know the devil is a lie!!!

Today know that God always has a plan. And what you're going through now is not in vain.

Remember, your affliction often reveals God's purpose for you.

For there is a time and a way for everything, even when a person is in trouble. (Ecclesiastes 8:6)

At the end of the day:

AUGUST 22

IT'S RAINING

When it pours, it rains, that is a saying that we have all heard at some point in our lives. It's usually said when one thing or another keeps taking place and it causes you to feel as if you are carrying an elephant on your back.

Today, know that if you are experiencing turmoil and pain in your life.... You should count it all joy because God is up to something! He is working behind the scenes on your behalf. The devil might be busy, but it just means that he knows that God has a blessing with your name on it and he is going to pull out every trick and scheme to keep your mind off Jesus.

Remember, trouble falls like rain and lately it's been pouring down, but He promised to never let it flood on you.

Shower, O heavens, from above, and let the clouds rain down righteousness; let the earth open, that salvation and righteousness may bear fruit; let the earth cause them both to sprout; I the LORD have created it. (Isaiah 45:8)

At the end of the day:

_____
_____
_____
_____
_____
_____
_____
_____

AUGUST 23

IT'S PAINFUL

People may not know when you laugh you are really trying to stop yourself from crying or they can't see the tears and pain behind your smile.

Today, be thankful for the hard times. The enemy might think that they have knocked you down.... and you are down.... But on your knees praying and crying out to God.

Remember, "the problem of pain meets its match in the scandal of grace." (Phillip Yancey)

He will wipe away every tear from their eyes, and death shall be no more, neither shall there be mourning, nor crying, nor pain anymore, for the former things have passed away. (Revelation 21:4)

At the end of the day:

_____
_____
_____
_____
_____
_____
_____
_____
_____
_____
_____

AUGUST 24

IT'S OUT OF CONTROL...BUT

Oftentimes when we look at our situation it can look dim and gloomy. Often making us depressed, dismayed and trying to pop every pill in sight ....to find an answer and a cure. In reality, we get out of control but God is still in control.

Today as bad as it looks and as bad as "they" told you it was. You have to know that the devil is a lie! No weapon formed against you will prosper. (Isaiah 54:17) GOD HAS THIS.

Remember, you have to keep trusting God, no matter what it looks like....because He is in control even when your circumstances seem out of control.

At the end of the day:

_____
_____
_____
_____
_____
_____
_____
_____
_____
_____
_____

AUGUST 25

IT'S NOT OVER

It might look as if things are looking mighty gloom and the enemy is winning. But things are not as bad as they seem. Don't be discouraged by that bad medical report, how low the bank statement looks, what the lawyer said or even what "they" told you. "They" can say whatever they want...but we know that God will have the final say. (Proverbs 19:21)

Today you must hold your head up high and stop worrying about something that is already in God's hand! He has you! What the enemy means for evil, God will work it out for your good!!!! (Genesis 50:20)

Remember, it may look like you have lost the battle now...but just know that you haven't lost the Savior.

The enemy doesn't get the final say...God does. And He says, "I will cause YOU to triumph!" (2 Corinthians 2:14)

It's Not Over!

Despite all these things, overwhelming victory is ours through Christ, (Romans 8:37)

At the end of the day:

_____
_____
_____
_____
_____
_____
_____

AUGUST 26

IT'S NOT BY ACCIDENT

I know it's been difficult and I know it hurts! But you have to know it's not by accident that your circumstances have fallen the way they have. God has set this up for a reason.

Today is not the day to say, "why me lord...or I always have bad luck." Change the way you speak and say, "thank you Lord!" Because God has something great in store for you; but He needs to see how you can handle adversity. Are you going to curse Him and shut Him out? Or are you going to praise Him in the midst of the trial and storm.

Remember, what the enemy means for evil, God means for your good. But you have to count it all joy for the trials that you are suffering from. Because it is the testing of your faith that is producing your steadfastness. (Genesis 50:20) (James 1:2)

Many of you have heard of Job's perseverance and have seen what the Lord finally brought about. Never forget that!!!!!! The Lord is full of compassion and mercy!!!! So, it's imperative that you stay prayed up & encouraged and never ever give up!!!!!! (James 5:11)

So be truly glad. There is wonderful joy ahead, even though you have to endure many trials for a little while. (1 Peter 1:6)

At the end of the day:

_____
_____
_____
_____
_____

AUGUST 27

IT'S NOT A PUNISHMENT

Sometimes when a door has closed that we wanted or something didn't work out in our favor. We start to think that it's God's way of punishing us; and that's just not the case.

Today, don't look at it as Him punishing you but look at it as Him protecting You. God is always there keeping us away from all harm. Don't lean unto your own understanding, but put your trust in The Lord; and He will direct your steps. (Proverbs 3:5-6)

Remember, this trial you're in is not a punishment; it's training. What has served its purposes is done. And God is doing what is best for us. He is training us to live God's Holy best! (Hebrews 12:7, 10)

For, He does not willingly bring affliction or grief to anyone. (Lamentations 3:33)

At the end of the day:

AUGUST 28

IT'S NECESSARY

Count it all joy when you are facing trials of various kinds. (James 1:2) Don't trip... that's what the enemy is wanting you to do. He is waiting and counting on your reaction to be hostile, frantic and in panic-attack mode. But we know God doesn't give us a spirit of fear...so the devil is a lie! (2 Timothy 1:7)

Today, know that it's necessary for you to face your "Goliath". It's necessary that you face your demons. It's necessary that you forgive that sister or brother that has hurt you. It's necessary that you let "it" go. It's necessary that you move forward.

Remember, it's necessary that you know that God will be your provider, shield, rock, protector and your all and all.

It's necessary that you continue to stand and let the will of God prevail!

At the end of the day:

_____
_____
_____
_____
_____
_____
_____
_____
_____

AUGUST 29

IT'S JUST A TEST

Our Faith is tested daily...Satan is always at work. When trials and tribulations come, that's the time for your Faith to shine.

Today, pass the test! Don't get angry, mad, bitter and want to seek revenge. But pass the test and let God take you to a new level. God is fighting your battles...all you have to do is be still and have Faith.

These trials will show that your faith is genuine. It is being tested as fire tests and purifies gold. (1 Peter 1:7)

At the end of the day:

AUGUST 30

IT'S HOT IN HERE

When you are going through- sometimes it feels as if you are Shadrach Meshach and Abednego in the fiery furnace all over again. (Daniel 3: 1-30) You're hot literally and you feel as if everything in your life is hot and a hot mess. But thank God for His grace and mercy.

Today know that if The Lord has brought you to it ... He surely will bring you through it.

Remember, it's time to turn into a teabag. Why? Because you never know how strong you are until you get in the "hot" water.

At the end of the day:

_____
_____
_____
_____
_____
_____
_____
_____
_____
_____
_____
_____
_____
_____
_____
_____

AUGUST 31

IT'S HIS WILL THAT YOU FACE IT

God knows that you are hurting. Make no mistake about the fact that He sees, hears and delivers!!! (Psalm 34:17) The question can't be why is this happening to me? But now the question needs to be, "God let Your will be done."

Today, you need to know that it was God's will that David faced Goliath. It was God's will that Moses came head to head with Pharaoh. Now it's God's will that you face your circumstance(s). Stop asking, "when will it end But start asking God, "how can I mature while I'm in it?"

Remember, it is God's will that you face it. You can't see it now...but soon and very soon you will see and understand why. And just like the bread... God will break, bless and multiply YOU! (Luke 24:30)

He has delivered us from such a deadly peril, and He will deliver us again. On Him we have set our hope that He will continue to deliver us, (2 Corinthians 1:10)

At the end of the day:

_____
_____
_____
_____
_____
_____
_____
_____

SEPTEMBER 1

IT'S HIS PROMISE

The tears, pain, heartache, woes, trouble, drama, trauma, hurt and loneliness can be hard to bear. But God has made promises to YOU! With that said, you must know that life is hard…but it is still worth living for.

Today, God's plans and promises for you are still here. He hasn't forgotten about them or you. His plans are magnificent for your life. It's something that you can't even begin to fathom. (Jeremiah 29:11)

His promises have kept and are continually keeping you! You haven't lost your mind and depression isn't weighing you down…God is and will always step right in when you need Him the most. YOU are safely in His arms! (Deuteronomy 33:27)

Remember, He gives power to the weak and strength to the powerless. Even youths will become weak and tired, and young men will fall in exhaustion. But those who trust in the Lord will find new strength.

They will soar high on wings like eagles. They will run and not grow weary. They will walk and not faint. (Isaiah 40:29-31)

And because of his glory and excellence, he has given us great and precious promises. (2 Peter 1:4)

At the end of the day:

_____
_____
_____
_____

SEPTEMBER 2

IT'S HANDLED

Some days life's overwhelming challenges can consume you where you just feel like you can't take another blow. If your life was a movie it would be titled, "Straight Out of My Mind"

Today what feels like it is too much is just the enemy's way of trying to confuse you. You have to know that God never gives us more than we can handle. But He does help us handle what we are given.

So, remember, you are not going out of your mind and you're not going to lose it. God is going to help you handle it all!

YOU are a soldier...and He gives His hardest battles to His toughest soldiers! (You got this)

And God is faithful; he will not let you be tempted beyond what you can bear. But when you are tempted, he will also provide a way out so that you can endure it. (1 Corinthians 10:13)

At the end of the day:

_____
_____
_____
_____
_____
_____
_____
_____
_____

SEPTEMBER 3

IT'S GETTING ROUGH

Although the wind blows and the storms tarry. You still won't crumble. (Matthew 7:25)

Today you need to know that it might get rough for a moment but God is in for the long haul. His Word tells us that He will not leave nor forsake us. (Deuteronomy 31:6)

Remember, you CAN & you WILL make it through this storm. You are not built to break. God will see you through!

HOLD ON!!!!!

Though the mountains be shaken and the hills be removed, yet my unfailing love for you will not be shaken nor my covenant of peace be removed," says the LORD, who has compassion on you. (Isaiah 54:10)

At the end of the day:

_____
_____
_____
_____
_____
_____
_____
_____
_____
_____

SEPTEMBER 4

IT'S FOR A REASON

Sometimes it's hard understanding why things are happening when they are, or why the door you thought was opened, closed suddenly.

Today, lean not unto your own understanding but trust in The Lord. (Proverbs 3:5) Whether you know it or not God, has a reason for it.

Remember, we may never understand His wisdom, but we have to trust His will!

Delight yourself in the Lord, and He will give you the desires of your heart. Commit your way to the Lord; trust in him, and He will act. He will bring forth your righteousness as the light, and your justice as the noonday. (Psalm 37:4-6)

At the end of the day:

_____
_____
_____
_____
_____
_____
_____
_____
_____
_____
_____
_____

SEPTEMBER 5

IT'S CALLED A FIERY TRIAL

If you are under attack that is because you have blessing in the inside of you that God is about to birth out that is so big, that the devil has to shut and take you out by any means necessary. Don't worry brothers and sisters it is what we call a fiery trial. The good news is God has a plan for you. He knew that you were going to be attacked. Unlike you right now, He is not somewhere tripping. He has already laid out the design plan to position and bless you. He is even taking care of the enemy that is wronging you.

Today, you need to know that God is in control. You are going to be on FIRE for the Lord and let Him work it out for you. He is quite aware of your situation and is working and walking it out for you. All you need to do is be still and let Him go to work.

So... sit back, relax, release and chill. Your Daddy has YOU!

Beloved, do not be surprised at the fiery ordeal among you, which comes upon you for your testing, as though some strange thing were happening to you; but to the degree that you share the sufferings of Christ, keep on rejoicing, so that also at the revelation of His glory you may rejoice with exultation. If you are reviled for the name of Christ, you are blessed, because the Spirit of glory and of God rests on you. (1 Peter 4:12-14)

At the end of the day:

_____
_____
_____
_____

SEPTEMBER 6

IT'S BEEN HARD

No matter what you are going through, God has given you the power and strength to face it. Not only have you confronted the storm but you are dealing with it.

Today you need to know that all the devastating news you've been hit with, and the trials that have come your way...were designed to make you stronger!

Remember, you've survived the toughest, hardest and most chaotic storms of your life....but, you're still standing!

We are pressed on every side by troubles, but we are not crushed. We are perplexed, but not driven to despair. We are hunted down, but never abandoned by God. We get knocked down, but we are not destroyed. (2 Corinthians 4:8-9)

At the end of the day:

_____
_____
_____
_____
_____
_____
_____
_____
_____
_____
_____

SEPTEMBER 7

IT'S ALREADY DONE

You have been crying, standing and praying for God to move in your life. Day in and out you think that you have been forgotten about; but, that just isn't the case. God knows every single hair on your head. Don't be afraid; you are worth more than many sparrows. (Luke 12:7)

Today whatever you have been needing God to do for you, it's already done. No matter how hard you think it is, know it's a done deal!

For by grace you have been saved through faith. And this is not your own doing; it is the gift of God. (Ephesians 2:8)

You are going to be just fine!!!!!

Fear not, little flock, for it is your Father's good pleasure to give you the kingdom. (Luke 12:32)

At the end of the day:

_____
_____
_____
_____
_____
_____
_____
_____

SEPTEMBER 8

IT'S A PROCESS

You might be feeling as if life has left your body. The pain, hurt and heartache is too much to bear. But God needs you to know that none of what you're going through will be in vain....it had to happen!!!

Today know that all you are going through is just a process to get you to your promise; of which God is going to get the glory from. It's about the release, courage, unveiling, wisdom, and growth. YES....it may be slow but quitting won't speed it up!

Remember, coffee is just grounds until it goes through the hot water!

TRUST THE PROCESS!

And it came to pass in process of time, (Exodus 2:23)

At the end of the day:
___
___
___
___
___
___
___
___
___
___
___
___

SEPTEMBER 9

IT'S A MOVING SITUATION

You don't need Two Men and a Truck, Mayflower, Atlas Van Lines or U-Haul to move things in your life.

Today, know that God will and is moving things on your behalf. It may look as if nothing is happening, but just because you don't see a way doesn't mean that God isn't making a way!!!

Remember, God doesn't move in your life when you struggle. He moves when you pray!

Do not be anxious about anything, but in everything by prayer and supplication with thanksgiving let your requests be made known to God. (Philippians 4:6)

For in Him, we live and move and have our being; as even some of your own poets have said, For we are indeed his offspring (Acts 17:28)

At the end of the day:

SEPTEMBER 10

IT'S A BATTLE

The enemy comes for you....and he wants to take, steal, destroy, control and even kill. (John 10:10) But thank God, we know the devil is a lie! Because the battle doesn't belong to us, but to The Lord!

Today recognize that you are going through a battle. But this storm, trial and test won't take you out.

Remember, every battle is won before it is ever fought! (Sun Tzu)

This is what the LORD says: Do not be afraid! Don't be discouraged by this mighty army, for the battle is not yours, but God's. (2 Chronicles 20:15)

At the end of the day:
_____
_____
_____
_____
_____
_____
_____
_____
_____
_____
_____
_____
_____
_____

SEPTEMBER 11

IT'S YOUR DUE SEASON

I know the pain that you are going through right now because things have gone sour and you didn't expect to be here right now in your life. But God has a plan. He knows that you are filling your pillow with tears at night. He knows you're drinking like a fish. He knows that you are having thoughts of suicide. He knows that you feel like no one understands. He knows that your spouse is cheating. He knows that your family and friends have abandoned you. But God said for you to hold on. He is about to shift and turn the tables. He needs you to be faithful just a little longer.

Today, don't give in to the enemy. God is looking at how you are handling this. He wants to know that if he strips everything from you like Job, will you curse Him or praise Him? Show Him that you will still be a faithful servant and praise Him all the way through to your victory.

Remember, it won't rain forever. The sun will come out. Just keep holding the umbrella up just a little longer. Because the Son is getting ready to shine upon YOUR life!

The Lord bless you and keep you; The Lord make His face shine upon you, And be gracious to you; The Lord lift up His countenance upon you, And give you peace. (Numbers 6:24-26)

At the end of the day:

_____
_____
_____
_____
_____

SEPTEMBER 12

IT'S THE WORST

What you are going through now is the worst storm that you've ever been in. You just want to tell God, "If it's got to go down like this, WELL FINE...but can't you at least give me a heads up!

Well today is the day that you need to know that it may appear to be the worst storm of your life, but looks can be deceiving. God is using this to stretch you. So, stop being a prisoner and trust the architect of your future.

Remember, it's not the worst...but it's for the better!

Weeping may endure for a night, but joy cometh in the morning. (Psalm 30:5)

At the end of the day:

_____
_____
_____
_____
_____
_____
_____
_____
_____
_____
_____
_____
_____

SEPTEMBER 13

IT'S THE JOY YOU HAVE

You've been through devastation, pain, heartache and loss after loss. But as much as the enemy tries to take, steal and kill.... (John 10:10) he can't take your joy!

Today, don't worry and shed another tear about the job, marriage, relationship and materialistic loss that you've suffered. God is going to give you back everything that was taken unlawfully. (Joel 2:25)

Remember, the joy you have, the devil didn't give it to you and he can't take it from you. You got joy and it's within YOU....not in things, people or a place.

These things I have spoken to you so that my joy may be in you, and that your joy may be made full. (John 15:11)

At the end of the day:

_____
_____
_____
_____
_____
_____
_____
_____
_____
_____
_____

SEPTEMBER 14

IT'S PREPARING YOU

With everything that you are going through, you probably feel as if you are alone. But that is what the devil wants you to think. He wants you to feel isolated and to think no one cares.

Today, you need to know that someone does care and that is God. (1 Peter 5:7) He is never going to let the righteous be shaken or His children to be begging for bread. (Psalm 37:25) All that you have endured is just setting you up for your biggest and greatest blessings.

Remember, count it all joy for this trial that you are enduring. Because this testing of your faith is producing endurance! (James 1:2-3)

We give great honor to those who endure under suffering. For instance, you know about Job, a man of great endurance. You can see how the Lord was kind to him at the end, for the Lord is full of tenderness and mercy. (James 5:11)

At the end of the day:

_____
_____
_____
_____
_____
_____
_____
_____
_____

SEPTEMBER 15

IT'S NOT WASTED

Everything that you've been through was designed to make you stronger. God had to allow you to go through it so you could grow through it.

Today, know that no experience or life lesson that you've learned was wasted. The good, the bad, the ugly and even the painful ...God still used it all.

Remember, if you could look and see the blessing that God is about to pour out over your life. You will understand the magnitude of the battle that you had to face.

And the glory of the LORD will be revealed, and all people will see it together. For the mouth of the LORD has spoken.

At the end of the day:

_____
_____
_____
_____
_____
_____
_____
_____
_____
_____
_____

SEPTEMBER 16

IT'S NOT TOO LATE

You might be in a panic and tripping, thinking that God has forgotten about you and it's too late for Him to do what he says He is going to do. But just hold tight because in just a little while, He who is coming will come and will not delay. (Hebrews 10:37)

Today, hold your head up high and don't be anxious about what is going on in your life. If God said it, He will definitely do it! He keeps His promises and He is faithful. Keeping His covenant of love to a thousand generations of those who love Him and keep His commandments. (Deuteronomy 7:9)

Remember, God is always on time. He is never behind and never ahead. Happy is the person who learns to wait as he/she prays. For God's time is always the best time!!!

For the revelation awaits an appointed time; it speaks of the end and will not prove false. Though it lingers, wait for it; it will certainly come and will not delay. (Habakkuk 2:3)

At the end of the day:

_____
_____
_____
_____
_____
_____
_____
_____

SEPTEMBER 17

IT'S NOT THAT SERIOUS

This week it seemed like I encountered a rude sales person, waiter, attendant or clerk every day. I get that we all have bad days and sometimes wake up on the wrong side of the bed, but every day? I had to stop, mediate, pray and realize that it's no one but that ugly little devil trying to get my focus off my God!! Which brings me to my topic, it's not that serious!!!!

Luke 6:38 reads, "Give, and it shall be given unto you;" God gave His best by sending Jesus. We are to gratefully seek to serve Him, and give Him the best that we have. In 1 Corinthians 13:5, "Love does not behave rudely", and the Greek word for rude means shameful or disgraceful behavior. Do we have to be rude, nasty or ugly to one another? It's not that serious!!! The world that we live in now is absolutely crazy. There are countless images from social media websites, TV, Internet, and Billboards that we just don't have any control over, but WE CAN control what we focus on. So, focus on a lifestyle that's pleasing to God and leading to a more rewarding life.

Today, know that we are people of God. We must strive to be the best, and do the best. For He made everything very good and we must focus on things that are worthy of praise. We are called to think about and focus our thoughts on these things. Now That Is Serious!!!!!!!!!!!

Finally, brethren, whatsoever things are true, whatsoever things are honest, whatsoever things are just, whatsoever things are pure, whatsoever things are lovely, whatsoever things are of good report; if there be any virtue, and if there be any praise, think on these things. (Philippians 4:8)

At the end of the day:

SEPTEMBER 18

IT'S NOT IMPOSSIBLE

God can do all things and no purpose of His can be thwarted. (Job 42:2) What is impossible with man is possible with God. (Luke 18:27) There is nothing too hard for God to do for you. For no word from God will ever fail. (Luke 1:37)

Today don't worry about your life; whether it is food, clothes, finances, a place to live or transportation. Look at the birds of the air; they do not sow or reap or store away in barns, and yet your heavenly Father feeds them. Are you not much more valuable than they? (Matthew 6:25-34)

You are God's Child and You will not want for anything (Psalm 23:1)

Abba, Father, he said, "everything is possible for you. Take this cup from me. Yet not what I will, but what you will." (Mark 14:36)

At the end of the day:

_____
_____
_____
_____
_____
_____
_____
_____
_____
_____

SEPTEMBER 19

IT'S NOT FAIR

I had someone tell me before that had done me very wrong that, "oh well, life isn't fair." I mean let's face it, we live in a world where things happen all the time that is unfair.

Recently, I had a conversation with a pastor and we were discussing how life's circumstances can cause people to not want to come to church anymore. They start to question God because they have been dealt a bad hand. No matter how many times they get up, they still get knocked down. Then they start to think that God is forgetting about them and not answering their prayers and cries for help. Sadly, they have it all wrong. God is close to the broken hearted and He hears their cries.

The LORD is close to the brokenhearted and saves those who are crushed in spirit. (Psalm 34:18)

At the end of the day:

___
___
___
___
___
___
___
___
___
___

SEPTEMBER 20

IT'S NOT AN OPTION

The winds and storms have been tarrying in your life and wreaking havoc with a vengeance. However, you continue to give God all the praise and glory because you know He is the source to why you are still standing. Fact is...quitting is just not an option.

Today recognize that, although the weapons and storms formed, God still didn't allow it to touch and cause you harm. (Isaiah 54:17) It's time to decide that giving up and out just won't be a choice.

Remember, what you can become, depends upon what you can overcome. (Anthony Douglas Williams)

Let us not become weary in doing good, for at the proper time, we will reap a harvest if we do not give up. (Galatians 6:9)

At the end of the day:

_____
_____
_____
_____
_____
_____
_____
_____
_____
_____
_____
_____

SEPTEMBER 21

IT'S HAPPENING FOR A REASON

Dear friends, the things that are happening to you right now, like the fiery trial that has you all in an uproar, please don't be surprised by them. I know it seems strange and you don't understand why this is happening to you. (1 Peter 4:12) But the Lord will come as he did against the Philistines at Mount Perazim and against the Amorites at Gibeon and He will come to do his work for your life. (Isaiah 28:21)

Today you need to know that everything happens for a reason. The door that got closed in your face, the divorce that caused you pain and that friendship that ended out of the blue is all for God to set you up for something greater. So be truly glad in this moment, because there is wonderful joy ahead; despite the fact of having to deal with various trials for a while.

Know that this storm will show that your faith is genuine and it is being tested as fire tests and purifies gold. Your faith is far more precious than mere gold. So, when your faith remains strong through this trial and the ones that will come later; it will bring you much praise, glory and honor on the day when Jesus Christ is revealed to the whole world. (1 Pet 1:6-7)

At the end of the day:

_____

_____

_____

_____

For it is God who works in you to will and to act in order to fulfill his good purpose. (Philippians 2:13)

SEPTEMBER 22

IT'S GOT TO GET DEEP

Going through the fire, storm and a turmoil season can be extremely difficult. It's hard seeing the light at the end of the tunnel...or better yet, seeing God working on your behalf.

Today, count it all joy for the pain that you are enduring. (James 1:2) Whether you know it or not there is a reason for everything that is taking place. And in this season... YOU will see that what was meant to hurt you will be God's very best for you! (Genesis 50:20)

Remember, the deepest level of worship is praising in spite of the pain.

Trusting God during your trial, surrendering while suffering, and loving Him when He seems distant. (Rick Warren)

God blesses those who are persecuted for doing right, for the Kingdom of Heaven is theirs. God blesses you when people mock you and persecute you and lie about you and say all sorts of evil things against you because you are My followers. Be happy about it! Be very glad! For a great reward awaits you in heaven. And remember, the ancient prophets were persecuted in the same way." (Matthew5:10-12)

At the end of the day:

___
___
___
___
___
___

SEPTEMBER 23

IT'S GOING TO MAKE YOU STRONGER

Everything that you have been through and in some cases going through now will make you stronger.

Today, don't focus on the circumstances that you see in front of you. Instead look to Jesus and keep your eyes on Him; He is the champion who initiates and perfects our faith. (Hebrews 12:2)

Remember, when it seems as if the waves are taking you under, hold on just a little bit longer, because God knows this is going to make you stronger!

Have I not commanded you? Be strong and courageous. Do not be frightened, and do not be dismayed, for the Lord your God is with you wherever you go. (Joshua 1:9)

At the end of the day:

_____
_____
_____
_____
_____
_____
_____
_____
_____
_____
_____
_____

SEPTEMBER 24

IT'S GOING TO BE OK

Thank God, it's Friday! Right? But I am sure a portion of you are saying you are still working tonight and tomorrow, so you don't agree. Well that is okay because God will still be covering you. I know it's hard to smile and get happy when things look so dim and gloomy, but guess what? God is still on His throne and no matter what it looks like, in a split of a second He can change your situation around. YOU are going to be okay.

Keep Praying, Keep Pushing and Keep Moving Forward on The Promises from God for Your Life!

God wants you to know that His grace is sufficient for you and His power works best in weakness. (2 Corinthians 12:9)

At the end of the day:

SEPTEMBER 25

IT'S GETTING ROUGH

When you are in the midst of a trial, it seems as if everything falls and drops at the same time. Overwhelming you and making the problems you are having to endure literally wear you out.

Today, you need to know that even though it's hard for you to get up out of bed and press on. You have to continue to fight through the bad days in order to get to the best days of your life.

Remember, yes, it's rough and yesterday was a bad day...but Thank God it is a bad day and not a bad life!

The Lord is a refuge for the oppressed, a stronghold in times of trouble. Those who know your name trust in you, for you, LORD, have never forsaken those who seek you. (Psalm 9:9-10)

At the end of the day:

_____
_____
_____
_____
_____
_____
_____
_____
_____
_____

SEPTEMBER 26

IT'S BEHIND YOU, NOW LOOK AHEAD

Many of you have been through some stormy weathers lately. If you probably talk about it, it might make you cry. But thanks, be to God that those days are behind you and He is springing up something new in your life!

Today, forget about the past and keep looking forward to what lies ahead. God has brought you a mighty way. Whether you know it or not, He is making a way. It may feel like you are living in a desert, but He is making streams in the wasteland. (Isaiah 43:19)

Remember, your yesterday is history, tomorrow is a mystery and today is a gift; which is why it is called "present".

At the end of the day:
_____
_____
_____
_____
_____
_____
_____
_____
_____
_____
_____
_____
_____
_____

SEPTEMBER 27

IT'S ALWAYS SOMETHING

There are days that you feel like you are, "sick and tired of being sick and tired." Every time you turn around, you are robbing Peter to pay Paul. Ducking and dodging bullets from the enemy. When bad news hits, all you can say is, "it's always something."

Fact is there is going to be something all the time and that is God. That's why the devil keeps coming in all directions and in different forms. He knows the blessings that are on your life and he wants to take you out...but the devil is a lie!

Today it might be a lot taking place and its overwhelming. But you need to know that it is God who is up to something. Because if He wasn't, the devil wouldn't be coming for you so hard.

Remember, the strength of patience hangs on our capacity to believe that God is up to something good for us in all our delays and detours. (John Piper)

See, God has come to save me. I will trust in Him and not be afraid. The LORD God is my strength and my song; H has given me victory. (Isaiah 12:2)

At the end of the day:

_____
_____
_____
_____
_____
_____

SEPTEMBER 28

IT'S ALL GOOD

Life can be hard, but it is worth living for. Don't let life's troubles and circumstances get you down. At the end of the day, you must keep pressing and moving forward.

Today, keep your head up and know that it's not only all good, but that it's all God.

Remember, if God brought you to it, He will bring you through it.

Stay Prayed Up & Encouraged ~

I press on toward the goal for the prize of the upward call of God in Christ Jesus. (Philippians 3:14)

At the end of the day:

_____
_____
_____
_____
_____
_____
_____
_____
_____
_____
_____
_____

SEPTEMBER 29

IT'S ALL GOOD

In life, you will be tested. There will be drastic changes that you didn't see coming. There will be promises that will be delayed and prayers that seem as if they are being unanswered. But through it all...God still works all things together for the good of those who love Him. (Romans 8:28)

Today tell yourself, "It's all good, the enemy can't and won't take me out." You have to know that YOU are from God and have already overcome them.

Because HE who is in you, is greater than he who is in this world. (1 John 4:4)

Remember, it's all good because it's all God!

At the end of the day:

_____
_____
_____
_____
_____
_____
_____
_____

"And those he predestined, he also called; those he called, he also justified; those he justified, he also glorified." (Romans 8:30)

SEPTEMBER 30

IT'S ABOUT WHERE YOU ARE GOING

The enemy comes for us because he knows that God has something great in store. That is why he fights so hard. You have to know that thieves don't rob empty vaults…they go after big loaded ones. There is no need for them to steal empty ones because there is nothing in them, but they know the ones that are loaded are full of "gems and diamonds". So, they target and hit them when you least expect it.

Today, you need to know that the enemy is fighting you, not because of where you are, but because of where God is taking you. He has big plans for your future, and they are not of evil, but to give you a future and a hope. (Jeremiah 29:11) You have to keep standing, because God is going to take you places that you didn't even dream of.

Remember, God has amazing plans just for YOU!!!! So, keep praying for direction to follow them, the patience to wait on them, faith to believe on them and the knowledge to know when they will come. He delights in every detail of your life! (Psalm 37:23)

The Lord of Hosts Himself has planned it; therefore, who can stand in its way? (Isaiah14:27)

At the end of the day:

_____
_____
_____
_____
_____

OCTOBER 1

IT'S A SPIRITUAL THANG

You might be going through marital issues and your spouse could be getting on your last nerve. Your child could be acting a fool. Your boss could be tripping in his or her role on the job. You got more bills than you do money. Due to the overwhelming things going on in your life, your health starts to deteriorate. You might be thinking, "Why me Lord? Why are "they" doing this to me?"

You have to realize that it is a spiritual battle that you're facing when you get hit all at once. As much as you want to blame people, they are never the true source of the problem; it is the forces of darkness that's the real problem.

You must know who is inside of you and who is giving you the strength and the power to overcome. You belong to God, my dear children. You have already won the victory over those people, because the Spirit who lives in you is greater than the spirit who lives in the world." (1 John 4:4)

At the end of the day:

_____
_____
_____
_____
_____
_____
_____
_____

OCTOBER 2

IT WON'T RAIN FOREVER

Saying you are a person of Faith doesn't exempt you from difficulties. The enemy may hit you with his best shot, but you need to remember that your house is built on the rock of Jesus. It won't rain forever and the storm will pass and you will come out stronger, victorious, increased, promoted and better off than you were before!

For by grace you have been saved through faith. And this is not your own doing; it is the gift of God, (Ephesians 2:8)

At the end of the day:

_____
_____
_____
_____
_____
_____
_____
_____
_____
_____
_____
_____
_____
_____

OCTOBER 3

IT WON'T LAST

What you are in and currently facing is not the end of the world. You need to know that trouble doesn't last always.

Today, tell the enemy, "You might have shaken and rattled me for the moment, but it won't last." I know who I belong to. And greater is He that is in me than He that is in the world." (1 John 4:4)

Remember, our Father is King and He is God. Your situation and problem is temporary, but God is eternal.

For our present troubles are small and won't last very long. Yet they produce for us a glory that vastly outweighs them and will last forever. (2 Corinthians 4:17)

At the end of the day:

_____
_____
_____
_____
_____
_____
_____
_____
_____
_____
_____
_____
_____
_____

OCTOBER 4

IT WON'T BE ME

We know that the devil comes at us like a roaring lion. (1 Peter 5:8) It's a fact. So, with that being said we have to fight this thing the only way we know how to fight. On our knees in prayer. Opening our mouth with praise and staying in the word of God.

Today you need to know that this is not the time for us to be sitting on the floor in a fetal position crying or lying in bed depressed...but it's time to say, "Okay, if it has to be like this, well let's get it on! Because, I'm ready to fight!" Tell the enemy, "I'm not going down like this!" Refuse to go down! Declare and decree, someone is going down, but it won't be me!

Remember, you are braver because you've fought giants and won. You are stronger because you had to be. You stand taller because you've survived through the storm.

Now then, stand still and see this great thing the LORD is about to do before your eyes! (1 Samuel 12:16)

At the end of the day:

___
___
___
___
___
___
___
___
___

OCTOBER 5

IT WAS DISAPPOINTING

You may have been disappointed and have had setbacks after setbacks. But not only is it all good, but it's okay.

Today know that everything that has hurt and caused you pain was actually a set up for God to redirect your life. So, what it didn't work out...God is still in control.

Remember, this setback is really your comeback...and you haven't seen nothing yet!

And hope does not put us to shame, because God's love has been poured into our hearts through the Holy Spirit who has been given to us. (Romans 5:5)

At the end of the day:

_____
_____
_____
_____
_____
_____
_____
_____
_____
_____
_____
_____
_____

OCTOBER 6

IT TAUGHT YOU

It's easy to get upset and caught up in what happened in your past. I get it...it hurts, It's not right, it's not fair; but it's not for you to avenge. Let God work it out!

Today, look at what has happened to you as a lesson learned. So what "they" think they have gotten the best of you. Let them keep on thinking that. You have to know that many are the plans in one's mind, but it is the purpose of the Lord that will always stand! (Proverbs 19:21)

Remember, one day this will be as if it never was; and you will look back at your life and thank God for it, because it taught you.

Sometimes you have to be broken to be blessed ~

At the end of the day:

OCTOBER 7

IT TAKES ONE STEP

Life can be just like a roller coaster. You are going to have your ups, downs, twists and turns. But you can't let what happens to you define you.

Today you need to know that all it takes is a small step to lead you in the right direction. Stepping out on faith and taking the first step will end up being the biggest step of your life.

Remember, faith is taking the first step, even when you don't see the whole staircase. (Dr. Martin Luther King Jr.)

For we walk by faith, not by sight. (2 Corinthians 5:7)

At the end of the day:

OCTOBER 6

IT WILL WORK OUT

You might have had fantastic plans for your life and in the blink of an eye, everything that you wanted was no longer. Making you feel depressed, battle weary and empty.

Today you need to know that even though what you wanted failed; it doesn't mean that God doesn't have great plans for your life. "This" is going to work out!

Remember, God's plans are always better than what you thought and they are bigger than your dreams. Just because you can't see it now, know that it will be rewarding and fulfilling.

Trust His Will!

For I know the plans I have for you," declares the LORD, "plans to prosper you and not to harm you, plans to give you hope and a future. (Jeremiah 29:11)

At the end of the day:

_____
_____
_____
_____
_____
_____
_____
_____
_____

OCTOBER 7

THE POWER OF GOD IS IN YOU

When you are feeling overwhelmed and daily challenges seem to overtake you, remember that as believers in Jesus and the same Spirit that raised Christ from the dead dwells in you! Today, rise up and declare and decree by Faith, "That I will be restored, healed... and everything that the devil tried to take, I'm getting back. The same spirit that raised Christ from the dead dwells in me!"

If the Spirit of Him who raised Jesus from the dead dwells in you, He who raised Christ Jesus from the dead will also give life to your mortal bodies through His Spirit who dwells in you. (Romans 8:11

At the end of the day:

_____
_____
_____
_____
_____
_____
_____
_____
_____
_____
_____
_____
_____
_____

OCTOBER 8

IT HAPPENED

Life happens. Divorce, heartache, pain, wins and losses. Good or bad, God already knew you were going to go through it.

Today, don't focus on what happened but focus on what's ahead. God does have a blessing with your name on it; but you can't get it if you're stuck in the past.

Remember, growth is painful. Change is painful, but nothing is as painful as being stuck somewhere you don't belong.

Look straight ahead, and fix your eyes on what lies before you. (Proverbs 4:25)

At the end of the day:

OCTOBER 9

IT HAD TO GET REAL

Sometimes, the very thing that hurts and feels like it is about to permanently take you out...Had to get that "real" to get your attention.

Today is the day that you can tell the devil, "It may have gotten real...but my God is real too!" You need to know that God will never take you to it without bringing you through it.

Remember, your struggle is real and you should be thankful for it; because without it you would have never stumbled across your strength. (Alex Elle)

What, then, shall we say in response to these things? If God is for us, who can be against us? (Romans 8:31)

At the end of the day:

_____
_____
_____
_____
_____
_____
_____
_____
_____
_____
_____

OCTOBER 10

IT HAD TO GET MESSY

All the turmoil, strife, pain and even affliction that you've had to deal with, was all for a reason. Yes, things are a mess and it's gotten dirty. But in the end...You'll see God's glory be revealed.

Today, face the fact that it's been a mess lately. But recognize that in order for the blessing to come, you had to deal with the mess.

Remember, sometimes messy is the necessary beginning to the making of extraordinary. (Michele Cushatt)

So keep watch at all times, and pray that you may have the strength to escape all that is about to happen and to stand before the Son of Man. (Luke 21:36)

At the end of the day:

_____
_____
_____
_____
_____
_____
_____
_____
_____
_____
_____

OCTOBER 11

IT FORMED, BUT

Weapons are going to be formed over your life. But you must thank God when they do. Because you know it won't prosper. (Isaiah 54:17)

Today recognize that the enemy is coming for you, because he knows the blessings over your life. But by the blood of Jesus…You are being protected from the North, South, East and West!

Remember, the enemy might try and "it" will form. But as long as you know God is for you…it won't touch you!

No weapon that is formed against you will prosper; And every tongue that accuses you in judgment you will condemn. This is the heritage of the servants of the LORD, and their vindication is from Me," declares the LORD. (Isaiah 54:17)

At the end of the day:

OCTOBER 12

IT DOESN'T LOOK GOOD

The situation that you are facing is probably overwhelming to you. In the natural, it doesn't look pretty at all. Somedays it's probably difficult to pray or even talk about it. But the devil is a lie!

Today, just because it doesn't look good doesn't mean that God isn't good!!! God is not only good but He is faithful! (Psalm 136:1) If you keep holding on to God's unchanging hand; He will change this thing in your favor. But you have to have faith!

Remember, God doesn't fail! It will all work out for your good! Never forget that nothing is impossible with God!   (Luke 1:37)

Stay Prayed Up & Encouraged ~

The Lord will grant that the enemies who rise up against you will be defeated before you. They will come at you from one direction but flee from you in seven. (Deuteronomy 28:7)

At the end of the day:

_____
_____
_____
_____
_____
_____
_____
_____
_____
_____

OCTOBER 13

IT DIDN'T BREAK YOU

You are about to walk and go into the best season of your life. Yes, the past few months have been hard but God heard and saw everything. He knows you have been faithful and your reward is getting ready to pay off.

Today know that what you went through didn't break you and because of it God has a breakthrough in store with your name on it.

Remember, the enemy meant it for evil but God is going to work it out for your good! (Genesis 50:20)

See, I am doing a new thing! Now it springs up; do you not perceive it? I am making a way in the wilderness and streams in the wasteland. (Isaiah 43:19)

At the end of the day:

_____
_____
_____
_____
_____
_____
_____
_____
_____
_____
_____

OCTOBER 14

IT COULD BE WORSE

Oftentimes when you are in the midst of a storm you can't even see God blessing and working in your life because all you are focused on is the disaster that you are caught up in. But God is aware of the suffering you have to endure. He wants you to pray and praise Him NOW! (James 5:13)

Today count it all joy while you are going through your trial. It is the testing of your faith that is producing steadfastness and developing you. (James 1:2-4) When it is all over you will know it was God and God only that rebuilt you.

Remember, God is not attracted to your problems but He is attracted to your praise.

So Get Your Praise On!

And we know that in all things God works for the good of those who love him, who have been called according to his purpose. (Romans 8:28)

At the end of the day:

___
___
___
___
___
___
___
___

OCTOBER 15

IT CAN COME UP MISSING

It's not only the thief/enemy that comes to steal and destroy; but there are people that are in your life that will want to take from you as well.

Today, you have to know that you have the right to be guarded. God wants you to live a life full of peace; so, that you may overflow with hope by the power of the Holy Spirit. (Romans 15:13)

Remember, when you allow the wrong people in your space, stuff will come up missing like; Joy, Peace, Love, Hope and Faith. YES...they steal these just as material things too!!!

Stay Prayed Up & Encouraged ~

Be on guard. Stand firm in the faith. Be courageous. Be strong. (1 Corinthians16:13)

At the end of the day:

_____
_____
_____
_____
_____
_____
_____
_____
_____

OCTOBER 16

IT AIN'T OVER, UNTIL GOD SAYS IT

Sometimes the enemy has a way of getting in your head. He will get you to believe the sun is actually green if you sit and listen to his foolishness long enough. You are probably saying to yourself, "Well I asked God about my situation and I feel He hasn't given me an answer yet." If that is the case you don't give in to the lies of Satan because God is silent. God always has a plan. If the enemy has you believing that you are all washed up and it's about to be over... Sit and hold tight because God is about to BLOW up your world!

Today, know that it doesn't matter what Satan is saying to you. He is not God. He has a sole purpose and that is to kill and destroy you. God has a plan to give you a future and a hope. Nothing that He will ever do to you is meant to harm you. Hold your head up and know that God said, "It ain't over."

Therefore, I will look to the Lord; I will wait for the God of my salvation; My God will hear me. Do not rejoice over me, my enemy; When I fall, I will arise; When I sit in darkness, The Lord will be a light to me. (Micah 7:7-8).

At the end of the day:

_____
_____
_____
_____
_____
_____
_____

OCTOBER 17

IS FEAR RULING YOU?

We all have fears of something or the other. Whether it is:

> Fear of making the wrong decision!
> Fear of rejection!
> Fear of not doing good!
> Fear of what others think!
> Fear of failure!
> Fear of moving forward! &
> Fear of the unknown!

Today, know that God has not given us a spirit of fear and timidity, but of power, love, and self-discipline. (2 Timothy 1:7) Declare & Decree right now that you will not walk in fear but in power!

You are God's Child...There is nothing to fear! TRUST, He has YOU!

When I am afraid, I put my trust in you. (Psalm 56:3)

At the end of the day:

_____
_____
_____
_____
_____
_____
_____
_____

OCTOBER 18

INTIMIDATE YOUR INTIMIDATOR(S) WITH PRAISE

The enemy wants you scared. His job is to steal, kill and destroy. (John 10:10) But thanks be to God, because He did not give us the spirit of fear, but of power, love and self-control. (2 Timothy 1:7)

Today, hold your head up high, put your shoulders back and walk like you know whose child you are. You belong to the most high God and there is no reason that you need to be scared or intimidated by anyone. Don't let the devil steal your joy!

Remember, the enemy is coming for you; because he knows God has something great for you! But The Lord is your strength and great defense! (Psalm 118:14)

As they began to sing and praise, The Lord set ambushes against the men of Ammon and Moab and Mount Seir who were invading Judah, and they were defeated. (2 Chronicles20:22)

So, Continue to Stay Prayed Up and Encouraged ~

At the end of the day:

_____
_____
_____
_____
_____
_____
_____

OCTOBER 19

INSANE FAITH

All you need is some insane crazy type of Faith for God to move and work in your life. He needs to know that you will step out on Faith and trust Him.

Today show God your insane crazy type of Faith. He needs to know that without a shadow of a doubt that even though with your natural eyes, it looks as if it is dead...but with your Faith; you know God can raise that dead situation up.

Remember, if you don't have faith it is impossible to please God. Because anyone who comes to Him must believe that He exists and that He rewards those who earnestly seek Him. (Hebrews 11:6)

For we live by faith, not by sight. (2 Corinthians 5:7)

At the end of the day:

OCTOBER 20

IN THE STORM

If you have ever been in a storm before, you know it isn't fun nor easy. You get scared and afraid of the disastrous outcome that it brings. When in reality, God is on control the whole time. There is a specific purpose for the storm that you can't see while it's raging toward you, but when it's over you will understand.

Today you need to know that God will not allow disaster to come at you that you can't handle or go beyond His boundaries. The storm will prove to be profitable if you submit to God.

Remember, when you endure severe pressure with unexplainable peace and joy, The Lord will confirm His Power; and in the end, YOU WILL come out victorious and a conqueror!

There will be a shelter to give shade from the heat by day, and refuge and protection from the storm and the rain. (Isaiah 4:6)

At the end of the day:

OCTOBER 21

IN THE END...YOU WIN

Looks can be deceiving and sometimes in the natural it can look as if you are in last place.

Just know that when the battle is over, you will win!

Today, God is working on your behalf. Those who were in last place just got moved to first place. (Matthew 20:16) {That's a shout que for someone right now} He is turning your situation around.

Remember, the battle is not yours but The Lord's!

The Lord will fight for you; you need only to be still. (Exodus 14:14)

Then you will win favor and a good name in the sight of God (Proverbs 3:4)

At the end of the day:

OCTOBER 22

IN HIS HANDS

Everyone has a problem or two that they want to try to fix. But it comes a time that you have to get wise and know that you need to put your life in the hands of the one who knows every single strand of hair on your head and the ins and outs of your life.

Today, trust His ways and not your own understanding.

And He took them up in his arms, put his hands upon them, and blessed them. (Mark 10:16 KJV)

At the end of the day:

OCTOBER 23

IN GOD'S TIMING

I know a lot of you are going through various trials, storms and major challenges in your lives right now and some of you may want to give up. But I encourage you to wait on God's timing. You need to know that right now as you are reading this, God is arranging all the pieces to work together for your good...BUT for His plan for your life. Believe it or not He has been working in your favor way before you even had the problem you are going through.

I pray that you and I (especially I) learn to grow patience and not try to force doors open. The answer will come, not on your time but in God's time!

For still the vision awaits its appointed time; it hastens to the end—it will not lie. If it seems slow, wait for it; it will surely come; it will not delay. (Habakkuk 2:3)

Stay Prayed Up & Encouraged ~

As Always, Sending Lots of Love & Blessings To All of You

At the end of the day:

_____
_____
_____
_____
_____
_____

OCTOBER 24

IN DUE TIME

A watched phone never rings. That is a saying I'm sure you have heard at some point in your life. We are a society that wants what we want when we want it. But God needs us to be patient and trust Him.

Today, know that your financial breakthrough is coming. The work that you need to get done is going to be completed. You will get over the one that has hurt you. The school work will lead to a degree. But you have to be patient and not get weary in well-doing. In due time, you will reap your harvest! (Galatians 6:9)

Remember, good things do come to those who wait, but better things come to those who are patient!

Be patient, then, brothers and sisters, until the Lord's coming. See how the farmer waits for the land to yield its valuable crop, patiently waiting for the autumn and spring rains. (James 5:7)

At the end of the day:

OCTOBER 25

I'M A GIANT KILLER

What you say is what you start to believe. If you walk around saying you are nothing, then you will be nothing. If you are walking around saying you are victorious, you will have the victory.

Today, don't let the enemy steal your joy. You are the head and not the tail. You are above and not beneath. You can tackle anything that is coming your way. You are a Giant Killer!

Death and life are in the power of the tongue, and those who love it will eat its fruits. (Proverbs 18:21)

At the end of the day:

OCTOBER 26

IF YOU ARE CONCERNED ABOUT IT...
HE CARES ABOUT IT

There may be a lot going on in your life. You could be feeling all alone, thinking no one cares. The devil is a lie!!!!

Today, know that God cares about everything that is a concern for you. He knows all about your pain, hurt, sorrow and tears. He is close to the brokenhearted and save those who are crushed in spirit. (Psalm 34:18)

Remember, He has a record of your misery, a list of every tear you have shed and all your sorrows have been tracked. He is going to take care of YOU!!!! (Psalm 56:8)

Fear not, stand firm, and see the salvation of the Lord, which he will work for you today. (Exodus 14:13)

At the end of the day:

_____
_____
_____
_____
_____
_____
_____
_____
_____
_____
_____

OCTOBER 27

IF HE DID IT BEFORE HE CAN DO IT AGAIN

I know many of you have lost a whole lot in 2017 and you are not sure how God is going to restore and rebuild you back to where you once were before. But I know a man who can do ALL THINGS! God will not leave you where you are. In the words of gospel recording artist

Tye Tribbett, "If He Did it Before, He Can Do it Again!"

Today set your hopes and dreams on high because this is your new season for restoration. EVERYTHING that the enemy tried to take and did take, God is getting ready to give it back to you and more. Sometimes you may have to lose in order to win.

Make room for your blessings because this is your season!

Instead of your shame you will receive a double portion, and instead of disgrace you will rejoice in your inheritance. And so, you will inherit a double portion in your land, and everlasting joy will be yours. (Isaiah 61:7)

At the end of the day:

_____
_____
_____
_____
_____
_____
_____
_____

OCTOBER 28

IF GOD CAN HEAR YOU HE WILL HEAL YOU

God will grant the desires of those who fear him, and He hears every cry and rescues those that are in distress and in trouble. (Psalm 145:19) The wicked must be aware though, because what they fear will indeed come; and the righteous prayers will be answered. (Proverbs 10:24)

Today don't focus on what the enemy is doing, but continue to cry out to The Lord. Keep on asking, seeking and knocking; the door will be open for you. (Matthew 7:7)

You shall weep no more. He will surely be gracious to you at the sound of your cry. As soon as He hears it, He answers you. (Isaiah 30:19)

At the end of the day:

_____
_____
_____
_____
_____
_____
_____
_____
_____
_____
_____
_____
_____

OCTOBER 29

I WILL FEAR NO EVIL

It can be hard not to feel afraid when you are being attacked. But we know that fear is not from God, it's from the enemy.

Today, hold your head up high, shoulders back and walk with confidence in knowing that God has a hedge of protection around you. There is nothing to fear. The Lord is standing right next to you like a mighty warrior. All of your persecutors that are coming at you will stumble. You will not be defeated. They will fail and thoroughly be put to shame and humiliated. Their dishonor will never be forgotten. (Jeremiah 20:11)

There is nothing to fear!

Even though I walk through the valley of the shadow of death, I will fear no evil, for you are with me; your rod and your staff, they comfort me. (Psalm 23:4)

At the end of the day:

_____
_____
_____
_____
_____
_____
_____
_____

OCTOBER 30

I WANT WHAT I WANT

Patience is something that a lot of people struggle with. Lord knows I do! Be careful of having the attitude and mindset that, "I want what I want when I want it and I want it now."

Today is the day that you need to know that what you want now, God already knows that it's not the best thing for you at this moment. So just hold tight and let Him work in His timing and not yours!

Remember, keep rejoicing in hope, be patient in tribulation and always be constant in prayer. (Romans 12:12) Trust, it will work out!

For the revelation awaits an appointed time; it speaks of the end and will not prove false. Though it lingers, wait for it; it will certainly come and will not delay. (Habakkuk 2:3)

At the end of the day:

_____
_____
_____
_____
_____
_____
_____
_____
_____
_____
_____

OCTOBER 31

I NEED TO BE

A lot of times we get so comfortable in saying what we need and what we need to do.

That we forget that life and death are in the power of the tongue. (Proverbs 18:21)

Today you have to quit saying:
You need to lose weight.
You need to find a job.
You need to find a good man or a good woman.
You need to put yourself on a budget.
You need to eat healthier.
You need to attend church on the regular.
You need to work out.
You need to mend that broken relationship.
You need to move on.

Fact is, what you need to do is put some faith and action to what you already know and actually act upon it!

Remember, the way to get started is to quit talking and begin doing (Walt Disney)

Anyone who listens to the Word but does not do what it says is like someone who looks at his face in a mirror and, after looking at himself, goes away and immediately forgets what he looks like. But whoever looks intently into the perfect law that gives freedom, and continues in it—not forgetting what they have heard, but doing it—they will be blessed in what they do." (James 1:23-25)

At the end of the day:

_____

_____

NOVEMBER 1

I HAVE TO

The enemy wants to take you out. He wants to raise havoc, hell, and chaos in your life. But what the enemy means for evil God is going to work out for your good! (Genesis 50:20)

Today you need to know that you have to stay in God's Word. You have to give Him praise. You have to pray. You have to find a bible-based, spirit filled church to worship Him in. You have to be obedient. YOU JUST HAVE TO!

Remember, obeying God sometimes seems like the hardest thing you can do. But in the end, it will give you undeniable joy and peace!

Why do you call me 'Lord, Lord,' and not do what I tell you? (Luke 6:46)

If you are willing and obedient, you shall eat the good of the land (Isaiah 1:19)

At the end of the day:

_____
_____
_____
_____
_____
_____
_____
_____
_____

NOVEMBER 2

I GOT THE POWER

When you have God in your life and acknowledge His greatness and start living by His word; He will do the exceedingly and abundantly above all that we can think, ask or imagine (Ephesians 3:20). You must know that we have been created by His image of The Almighty God. We have the power to do anything in Christ that strengthens us. (Philippians 4:13) Today know that the power lives in you every day because you are a child of the High Most God!

May you be strengthened with all power, according to his glorious might, for all endurance and patience with joy, (Colossians 1:11)

At the end of the day:

_____
_____
_____
_____
_____
_____
_____
_____
_____
_____
_____
_____
_____

NOVEMBER 3

I DON'T FEEL LIKE IT

Life can be so hard. You think that you are getting ahead and every time you turn around something keeps kicking you back down. Seasoned saints would say, "when it rains it pours."

I know you don't feel like praying. I also know that you are tired of going to church to be a seat filler because you feel so empty. You're sick and tired of crying and sick and tired of being sick and tired. The TV series Walking Dead is how you feel...a dead man/woman walking.

Today is the day that YOU need to know that even though you don't feel like it...God still hasn't taken His hands off of YOU! (Isaiah 41:13)

Remember, don't make these bad days make you feel like you have a bad life. Because even when you don't feel like it; that's when you have to keep on praying, pressing and pushing your way through!!!

Don't be afraid of what you are about to suffer. The devil will throw some of you into prison to test you. You will suffer for ten days. But if you remain faithful even when facing death, I will give you the crown of life. (Revelation 2:10)

At the end of the day:

_____
_____
_____
_____
_____
_____

NOVEMBER 4

HURT BUT NOT BROKEN

You might be hurt or brokenhearted by something or someone that has hurt or done you wrong. I get it! Your marriage has fallen, your child is acting a fool, you have lost your job, you have more bills than you do money, just got a bad medical report and now your ailing parent has taken a turn for the worse. All you can do now is say, "JESUS". Well the good news is God heals the broken-hearted. (Psalm 147:3) It may look and feel bad, but YOU ARE NOT BROKEN!

Today look to the hills where your help comes from because God is by your side through it all. (Psalm 121:1) He has promised to never leave you, nor forsake you. (Deuteronomy 31:6) You are going to make it through this.

Remember, do not get tired and faint not, but keep doing what is right and at the right time you will reap a harvest of blessings if you don't give up. (Galatians 6:9)

When the righteous cry for help, the Lord hears and delivers them out of all their troubles. The Lord is near to the brokenhearted and saves the crushed in spirit. Many are the afflictions of the righteous, but the Lord delivers him out of them all. He keeps all his bones; not one of them is broken. (Psalm 34:17-20)

At the end of the day:

_____
_____
_____
_____
_____

NOVEMBER 5

HOW BIG IS IT?

A lot of people now are going through some trying times and they feel like they just don't know what to do. But the one thing that they do is constantly talk about their problem. When they need to be talking about how big their God is instead.

Today, don't get so caught up in what you're going through but rather talk about how big your God is. Know that God has ordained you to do something great in this world. No matter what you are going through you must know that God is for you.

Do you not know? Have you not heard? The LORD is the everlasting God, the Creator of the ends of the earth. He will not grow tired or weary, and his understanding no one can fathom. (Isaiah 40:28)

At the end of the day:

NOVEMBER 6

HOLD YOUR PEACE

I know sometimes it is very hard to hold your peace when you are being accused and it looks as if the wicked is prospering over you. But the Lord says, "For you to be still and hold your peace and He will fight for you." (Exodus 14:14)

Today, know that The Lord laughs at the wicked because He knows their day is coming. (Psalm 37:13) So therefore, there is no need for you to trip and get dismayed over what you see in the natural. Yes, it might be unfair, but continue to hold your peace; because The Lord is fighting for you.

Remember, God is fighting your battles, arranging things in your favor and making a way... even though you can't see it right now!

For the LORD your God is the one who goes with you to fight for you against your enemies, to give you victory. (Deuteronomy 20:4)

At the end of the day:

_____
_____
_____
_____
_____
_____
_____
_____

NOVEMBER 7

HOLD ON TO GOD'S UNCHANGING HAND

What you are going through now can't even compare to what your later is going to look like. You must go through this test to have the testimony!

Today get your praise on because you don't look like what you are going through. If folks were attached to you and could see all the hell that you face and encounter daily; well they would have given up a long time ago. But YOU know that you weren't meant to break! So, keep holding on to God's unchanging hand.

Remember, God gives His hardest battles to His toughest and strongest soldiers. You may not know it but you are a soldier for The Lord!!! You already won the battle and victory is yours!

Stay Prayed Up

You have given me your shield of victory. Your right hand supports me; your help has made me great. Psalm 18:35

At the end of the day:

_____
_____
_____
_____
_____
_____
_____
_____

NOVEMBER 8

HOLD ON A LIL WHILE LONGER

What you are going through hurts. No one can take that away from you. The tears you cry, the heartache, the pain, the pacing in the middle of the night and pillow soaked full of tears is real. But my dear friend you can't give up now.

Today is the day that you hold on when you feel like you want to let go. God is a healer!!! He hears, He sees and He delivers!

Remember, you have to hold on without wavering; because God can be trusted to keep His promises!!! (Hebrews 10:23) Yes, it's rough and it's not what you planned, but you can get through this. You just have to hold on just a little longer and have the faith to know that better is coming!!!

Therefore do not throw away your confidence, which has a great reward. For you have need of endurance, so that when you have done the will of God you may receive what is promised. (Hebrews 10:35-36)

At the end of the day:

_____
_____
_____
_____
_____
_____
_____
_____

NOVEMBER 9

HIT HARD

The enemy might be coming at you like a flaming lightning bolt. I mean hitting you with his best shot. But guess what? You're still standing!

Today don't focus on how hard you've been hit by the lightening, but focus on how you are like a house built on the solid rock! (Matthew 7:24)

Remember, it's not about how hard you've been hit....but it's about how you can take the hit and keep pressing forward!

I press on to reach the end of the race and receive the heavenly prize for which God, through Christ Jesus, is calling us. (Philippians 3:14)

But the one who endures to the end will be saved. (Matthew 24:13)

At the end of the day:

_____
_____
_____
_____
_____
_____
_____
_____
_____
_____
_____

NOVEMBER 10

HIS POWER CAN GET YOU THROUGH

Your right hand, O LORD, is majestic in power, Your right hand, O LORD, shatters the enemy. (Exodus 15:6)

The Power of God is so magnificent that He can make a path through the Red Sea. (Exodus 14:21) He can take five loaves, two fish and feed thousands. (Matthew 14:19) I know that you are thinking, "that my situation is different I don't see how God can help me." But God!!!! There is nothing too hard or difficult that God can get you out of.

God's Power can get you out of anything. The pain, the hurt and the rejection is only temporary. God says lean on me, let me help you. I know you don't have the strength and I know you are about to give up, but old folks from the church used to say, "The trouble and heartache that you are in now is just a way of God letting you know that you are in a valley and He is preparing something mighty great for you!!!!!"

Your turnaround is so near that if you knew when it was going to take place you wouldn't be crying, worrying, drinking and your thoughts of suicide would cease. You must hold on. God is about to unleash so much Power on you and your situation that your enemies will start to tremble. When it's all said and done, you and others will know that it was God and Him only.

At the end of the day:

_____
_____
_____
_____
_____

NOVEMBER 11

HIS LIGHT IS STILL SHINING

We all are going to come into a time where it seems dark every day. Challenges, hard times and sorrow we will see. It's during these times that we must know that we are not alone. God is with us, even in the darkest stages of our lives.

Today, get ready to see God's light shining on your life. He is about to come bursting in like a dash of lightning to show you His power. God is getting ready to promote, restore and elevate you. When He is done showering you with His goodness everyone around you will know it was God that did it.

Get ready!

Even in darkness, light dawns for the upright, for those who are gracious and compassionate and righteous. (Psalm 112:4)

At the end of the day:

___

___

___

___

___

___

___

___

___

___

NOVEMBER 12

HE'LL PICK YOU BACK UP

You might have fallen and you might have gotten knocked down. But God is right here to pick you back up!

No matter how many times you have fallen or the enemy purposely pulled you down. God is picking and lifting you up today!!!

Remember, it's not about if or when you will get knocked down. But it's about how you get back up! (Vince Lombardi)

You may be down temporarily but God won't let you stay there!

For though the righteous fall seven times, they rise again, (Proverbs 24:16)

"Though they stumble, they will never fall, for the LORD holds them by the hand

At the end of the day:

NOVEMBER 13

HEELS HIGH....HEADS HIGH

But you, O LORD, are a shield around me; you are my glory, the one who holds my head high. (Psalm 3:3)

I know it can be very difficult at times to hold your head up when someone has done you wrong or has hurt you. Especially if you have been mistreated by a loved one, a spouse, someone you're in a relationship with, or even done foul by someone on your job. Let's face it...it hurts! I've come to learn though, that you must be quiet and be still and let go and let God!

Be still, and know that I am God; (Psalm 46:10)

Rest assure that by you turning your problems over to The Lord that you will find comfort and peace like no other. The enemy wants us to dwell on our problems and sit around and think about how we can get revenge and defend ourselves. But I promise you that is not the answer. You're not hurting anyone but yourselves and blocking your own blessing in the process. Your victory is found by turning your eyes to God.

At the end of the day:

_____
_____
_____
_____
_____
_____
_____

NOVEMBER 14

HE'S WORKING

When you are going through your storm, trial and even setback; it can be hard to see where God is in it. But you can believe...He is there.

Today you need to know that God is still working even though you can't see it in the natural. He is working behind the scenes on your behalf even at this very moment. He has never taken His hands off you.

Remember, it might hurt and doesn't feel too good at this time. But our present troubles are small and won't last very long. They will produce for us a glory that vastly outweighs them and will last forever! (2 Corinthians 4:17)

Yet what we suffer now is nothing compared to the glory he will reveal to us later. (Romans 8:18)

At the end of the day:

_____

_____

_____

_____

_____

_____

_____

_____

_____

_____

NOVEMBER 15

HE WILL RAISE YOU UP

When God is silent, that is when He is really working and will prove Himself to you. When Mary & Martha's brother Lazarus was sick and they asked Jesus to come and help him, He didn't come when they called on Him. In fact, He stayed gone for two more days. (John 11:6) They were hurt, devastated and confused. They couldn't understand why God would leave them like that. But when He did go, He not only healed but He raised Lazarus back up from the dead glorifying The Father. (John 11:11-15)

Today don't you get weary in well-doing. (Galatians 6:9) God has not forgotten about you. (Hebrews 6:10) He might not have answered your prayers yet, but He hears you. When He comes He won't just come and make things better for a little bit, but He is going to make things better for a lifetime.

These things you have done and I kept silence; You thought that I was just like you; I will reprove you and state the case in order before your eyes. (Psalm 50:21)

At the end of the day:

NOVEMBER 16

HE WILL END YOUR SUFFERING

When you are going through, it is hard to see how you are going to come out of it. You might be facing physical pain, heartache and heartbreak, or life struggles have just taken its toll on you. Remember it is not always what it looks like. You can't get weary in well-doing because God will indeed bless you with your harvest if you don't give up! (Galatians 6:9)

Today take comfort in knowing that after you have suffered a little while God Himself will restore, strengthen and establish you. (1 Peter 5:10) You might face many troubles day by day, but the Lord will deliver and rescue you every single time. (Psalms 34:19)

Blessed are those who have been persecuted for the sake of righteousness, for theirs is the kingdom of heaven. (Matthew 5:10)

At the end of the day:

_____
_____
_____
_____
_____
_____
_____
_____
_____
_____

NOVEMBER 17

HE WILL ALWAYS PROVIDE

God is nothing like man that He should lie. You best believe if He said it, He will do it! (Numbers 23:19) It's easy to get caught up and start to worry about your bills, your job, or what the outcome will be to the problem that you are having to endure for the moment. But if you will remain steadfast and hold on to His unchanging hand, All things will work out for you. (Romans 8:28)

Today be at peace knowing that no matter what you are going through, The Lord is faithful and He will keep His covenant with you. (Deuteronomy 7:9)

Remember, God is faithful and He will surely do it! (1 Thessalonians 5:24)

At the end of the day:

_____
_____
_____
_____
_____
_____
_____
_____
_____
_____
_____
_____
_____

NOVEMBER 18

HE WILL ACCOMPLISH HIS PURPOSE AND PROMISES

Things may look like in the carnal that it isn't looking all that good for you. But you must keep your eyes fixed on Jesus and not your situation. (Hebrews 12:2) God has said that He has great plans for your life and they are not to harm but to prosper you. (Jeremiah 29:11) God is not like man, He doesn't lie! When He says He is going to do something He will do it!!! He has never failed to act. (Numbers 23:19)

Today don't get so caught with what "it" looks like. God will accomplish what He desires and will achieve the purpose for which He sent it. (Isaiah 55:11) He is with you and watching over you wherever you go. He will not leave you until He has finished giving you everything He promised you. (Genesis 28:15)

My counsel shall stand, and I will accomplish all my purpose, (Isaiah 46:10)

At the end of the day:

_____
_____
_____
_____
_____
_____
_____
_____

NOVEMBER 19

HE USED IT

Everything that you are going through is not in vain. God has a way of using the pain, turmoil, hell, chaos and even the tears to work for your good.

Today, know that God is turning this thing around for you. What you thought would be your demise...is really your beginning and breakthrough.

Remember, does it say in the Bible figure it out? NO! But it does say over and over again to trust God. So trust Him.... Because He knows what He is doing and He is working this thing for your good.

Perhaps the LORD will notice my affliction and this day grant me good in place of his curse. (2 Samuel 16:12)

And we know that in all things God works for the good of those who love him, (Romans 8:28)

At the end of the day:

_____
_____
_____
_____
_____
_____
_____
_____
_____

NOVEMBER 20

HE SEES, HEARS AND WILL DELIVER

Through the pain, heartache, hurt and tears; God still has His hands on you. Yes, it's hard but God promises that He will never leave nor forsake you! (Deuteronomy 31:6)

Today, I know that it hurts like hell to keep pressing on; but count it all joy when you are enduring various trials. Because it is the testing of your Faith that produces steadfastness- James 1:2-3

Remember, don't worry because God is never blind to your tears, never deaf to your prayers and never silent to your pain. He sees, He hears and He will deliver!

Stayed Prayed Up & Encouraged

The righteous person may have many troubles, but the LORD delivers him from them all. (Psalm 34:19)

At the end of the day:

_____
_____
_____
_____
_____
_____
_____
_____
_____

NOVEMBER 21

HE SAVES THE BEST FOR LAST

It's easy to get caught up in this race called "life". Before you know it, you are looking back trying to see what the enemy is doing and what tricks he has up his sleeve. But don't be deceived, God is not mocked; for whatever a person sows they will surely reap. (Galatians 6:7)

Today don't focus on the enemy, but hold your head up and realize that your "now season" won't always be like this. God is getting ready to thrust you forward to your blessings and destiny. The race is almost over and even if you don't feel it, you are about to win!

Remember, those who are last now will be first, and those who are first will be last. (Matthew 20:16)

I have fought the good fight, I have finished the race, I have kept the faith. (2 Timothy 4:7)

At the end of the day:

_____
_____
_____
_____
_____
_____
_____
_____
_____

NOVEMBER 22

HE WILL RESTORE YOU

I know the Holidays can be difficult for lots of people, especially when you are going through a storm. The enemy just won't seem to leave you alone. Every day it seems as if you are dealing with something. I've learned that it just means your breakthrough is just around the corner.

See, satan has gotten a glimpse of what God is getting ready to do for you and he wants to take you out!!!! But today God has a mighty Word for you and He wants you to hang in there a little longer because your breakthrough is about to take place.

> Don't, cry!
> Don't get down!
> Don't throw in the towel!
> AND
> Don't quit!

God has many blessings with your name on it. So just Hold On!

"The Lord says, I will restore to you the years that the swarming locust has eaten, the hopper, the destroyer, and the cutter, my great army, which I sent among you. "You shall eat in plenty and be satisfied, and praise the name of the Lord your God, who has dealt wondrously with you. And my people shall never again be put to shame." (Joel 2:25-26)

At the end of the day:

_____

_____

_____

_____

NOVEMBER 23

THANKFUL

It's easy to say Happy Thanksgiving on the last Thursday of November and say what you are thankful for. But what about being thankful every day?

Today give thanks for all The Lord has done for you. Not just on one day of the year, but every day. The fact that you are up, breathing and reading this....is THANKSGIVING!

Remember, it's not about being thankful for what you got in prayer. But it is giving ten thousand thanks and beyond, for the countless blessings that God gave you without asking!

Have a Happy, Blessed & Safe Thanksgiving!

Giving thanks always and for everything to God the Father in the name of our Lord Jesus Christ, Ephesians 5:20

At the end of the day:

_____
_____
_____
_____
_____
_____
_____
_____
_____
_____

NOVEMBER 24

HE KEEPS HIS HANDS ON YOU

Life is hard but it is worth living for. Don't get dismayed in this season. The Lord your God takes a hold of your right hand and says to you, "Do not fear I am here to help you." (Isaiah 41:13) He has put YOUR name in the palm of His hand and your walls are forever before Him. (Isaiah 49:16)

Today you need to humble yourself under God's mighty hand, so at the right time He will lift you up in honor. (1 Peter 5:6) Your Father is more POWERFUL than anyone! It is imperative for you to know that no one can snatch you from His hands. (John 10:29)

So, continue to keep your eyes on The Lord because He is right beside you and you will not be shaken! (Psalm 16:8)

A Psalm of David. The LORD says to my Lord: "Sit at my right hand, until I make your enemies your footstool." (Psalm 110:1)

At the end of the day:

_____
_____
_____
_____
_____
_____
_____
_____
_____
_____

NOVEMBER 25

HE IS

When God places a promise in your heart, you have got to come to a place where you believe it's going to happen.

It may seem impossible, all the odds are stacked against you, but you know what God said and the promise that is within you. More importantly you know who He Is, and who is on the throne.

He is bigger than any obstacle or circumstance that you are facing.

He is working out the promise behind the scenes on your behalf.

He is the All Mighty One.

He is the image of the invisible God, the firstborn of all creation. (Colossians 1:15

At the end of the day:

_____
_____
_____
_____
_____
_____
_____
_____
_____
_____
_____
_____

NOVEMBER 26

HE IS STRENGTHENING YOU

A lot of times "life situations", trials and storms will wear a person down.

Making you feel like you don't have the strength to carry on. But the devil is a lie!

Today know that God is your strength that you have when you feel as if all hope is gone. He gives strength to the weary and increases the power of the weak. (Isaiah 40:29)

Remember, God is a God of STRENGTH...and He is strengthening YOU and you are becoming stronger because of it!

YOU will make it through this storm!

"But those who hope in the LORD will renew their strength. They will soar on wings like eagles; they will run and not grow weary, they will walk and not be faint." (Isaiah 40:31)

At the end of the day:

NOVEMBER 27

HE REIGNS

"But the LORD abides forever; He has established His throne for judgment, And He will judge the world in righteousness; He will execute judgment for the peoples with equity. The LORD also will be a stronghold for the oppressed, A stronghold in times of trouble; And those who know Your name will put their trust in You, For You, O LORD, have not forsaken those who seek You." (Psalms 9:7-10)

It's easy to get caught up in the "now" of life and get agitated and frustrated when you know things are wrong. Whether it's on your job, in relationships, or just in everyday life situations. People can be low down and life can throw you some hard blows but the one thing that I know for sure... God still reigns!

I had to remind myself this week that even though it looks and feels bad that God is still reigning. It's amazing how you think things are going to be one way and they have a way of turning out so left-field. I have always believed that God doesn't make mistakes. If you are somewhere in life it is because God has a reason and a purpose for you. Don't even question it. Remember, "Trust in The Lord with all your heart and lean not unto thy own understanding;" (Proverbs 3:5)

No matter what you are going through and facing today, know that God is FAITHFUL!

At the end of the day:
_____
_____
_____
_____

NOVEMBER 28

HE IS STILL WORTHY

With all that you have been going through, the pain, heartache and hell; God is still worthy of your praise!

Today, I know it's hard to get up and press through. But you must know that weeping may endure for a night, but joy will still come in the morning. (Psalm 30:5)

Remember, keep pushing until something happens!

Great is the LORD and most worthy of praise; his greatness no one can fathom. (Psalm 145:3)

At the end of the day:

___
___
___
___
___
___
___
___
___
___
___
___
___
___

NOVEMBER 29

HE IS STILL GOOD

You might have had some bad knocks, breaks and bad times in your life. But God has still been good to you.

Today, don't look and what has happened but focus on the good that God has been to you. He has never once left your side.

Remember, The Lord is so good and His faithfulness continues through all generations. (Psalm 100:5)

Give thanks to the Lord, for He is good, for His steadfast love endures forever. (Psalm 136:1)

At the end of the day:

_____
_____
_____
_____
_____
_____
_____
_____
_____
_____
_____
_____
_____
_____
_____

NOVEMBER 30

HE IS ALWAYS ON TIME

Often times when we are waiting for something to take place in our lives we tend to get impatient, especially if the clock is ticking and we don't know what to do. There is no need to worry because God is in the storm with you. He wants you to be strong and take courage but more importantly to wait for Him. (Psalm 27:14)

Today don't fret or worry about what is not getting done yet. Know that The LORD is good to those who wait for Him. So sit silently while waiting for your deliverance. (Lamentations 3:25-26) He will come right on time!

At the end of the day:

DECEMBER 1

HAVE A LITTLE FAITH

Sometimes all it takes is to have faith as small as a mustard seed to keep you going. (Luke 17:6) If you know in your heart that God is one you're going to make it. Even the demons believe this and they shudder. (James 2:19)

Today, know that the road may seem dark, gloomy and scary. But if you keep a little faith in God; He will see you through!

Remember, Faith is not hoping God can, it's knowing that He WILL!

And Jesus answered them, "Have faith in God. Truly, I say to you, whoever says to this mountain, 'Be taken up and thrown into the sea,' and does not doubt in his heart, but believes that what he says will come to pass, it will be done for him. Therefore, I tell you, whatever you ask in prayer, believe that you have received it, and it will be yours. (Mark 11:22-24)

At the end of the day:

_____
_____
_____
_____
_____
_____
_____
_____
_____
_____

DECEMBER 2

GREATER

Start thinking bigger, praying bigger and expecting bigger! This is a new day people… and God wants something bigger and better for you. He is taking you to a place you've never been before; but if you don't expect it, you will never see it.

Today open your heart and mind to greater for your life. God has plans for you and they are not for evil but to give you a future and a hope. (Jeremiah 29:11)

Remember, if you believe it, He will do it!

I eagerly expect and hope that I will in no way be ashamed, but will have sufficient courage so that now as always, Christ will be exalted in my body, whether by life or by death. (Philippians 1:20)

At the end of the day:

_____
_____
_____
_____
_____
_____
_____
_____
_____
_____
_____
_____

DECEMBER 3

GREATER IS COMING

When God says it, you have to believe it. He is not a man that he should lie. (Numbers 23:19) All of God's promises are being fulfilled for your life. That is why you should say Amen. (2 Corinthians 1:20)

Today, know that God has seen you be faithful over a few things... and now He is getting ready to make you a ruler of many. (Matthew 25:23) Because you have continued to take delight in The Lord, He is going to give you every desire of your heart. (Psalm 37:4)

So, sit back and enjoy the ride...your dreams are coming true!

And my God will supply every need of yours according to his riches in glory in Christ Jesus. (Philippians 4:19)

At the end of the day:

DECEMBER 4

GREAT IS HIS FAITHFULNESS

Every time when you are let down, dealing with a setback and life has thrown you some blows, remember that God is Faithful! People can hurt you, but Psalm 27:10 says, "Even if my father and mother abandon me, the LORD will hold me close."

Today, know that it might look as if things aren't going good in your life, and the enemy is winning. But the devil is a lie!!! God says, "He will never leave you nor forsake you."

Have Faith as small as a mustard seed and God will keep His promises to you!

He will not let the righteous be forsaken!

Know therefore that the Lord your God is God, the faithful God who keeps covenant and steadfast love with those who love Him and keep His commandments, to a thousand generations, (Deuteronomy 7:9)

At the end of the day:

_____
_____
_____
_____
_____
_____
_____
_____
_____

DECEMBER 5

GOT PROBLEMS...
GET MORE PRAISES

There is always going to be a problem that will arise in your life. How you deal with that will determine how big and long you will have the problem.

Today don't let the enemy see you sweat. Yeah, some hard knocks might have stumbled across your way. But you have the most powerful weapon on you to handle it, and that is a shout of praises from your mouth.

Remember, just turn it around; and let your praise be a problem for the enemy.

And now my head shall be lifted up above my enemies all around me, and I will offer in his tent sacrifices with shouts of joy; I will sing and make melody to the LORD. (Psalm 27:6)

At the end of the day:

_____
_____
_____
_____
_____
_____
_____
_____
_____

DECEMBER 6

GOT FAITH?

Don't walk around today and talk about your problems and talk about what you don't have and what you can't get. God did not call you to be a victim, but to be victorious! You must have faith as small as a mustard seed. Today you will choose to live with an attitude of greatness and expectancy.

Expect for God to do great wonders in your life.

Expect for God to make a way out of no way.

Expect for God to do the unseen and unthinkable that only He can.

Get your hopes up today and focus on God's goodness and faithfulness, and you will feel that hope inside of you start to grow.

He replied, because you have so little faith. Truly I tell you, if you have faith as small as a mustard seed, you can say to this mountain, Move from here to there, and it will move. Nothing will be impossible for you. (Matthew 17:20)

At the end of the day:

_____

_____

_____

_____

_____

_____

_____

DECEMBER 7

GOD'S DELAYS ARE NOT HIS DENIALS

When you are waiting on God to work in your life sometimes the waiting process can be hard. The trouble, worry and pain can weigh heavy on you. But you can't give up, because in due season, you will reap. (Galatians 6:9)

Today be strong and be of good courage while you wait patiently for The Lord to deliver you. (Psalm 27:14) There is a season and a time for every matter under Heaven. (Ecclesiastes 3:1)

Remember, He may not come when you want him, but He's always on time!

This vision is for a future time. It describes the end, and it will be fulfilled. If it seems slow in coming, wait patiently, for it will surely take place. It will not be delayed. (Habakkuk 2:3)

At the end of the day:

DECEMBER 8

GOD WILL WORK IT OUT

For anyone that is going through some trying times and some horrific storms. Know that you won't get out of your situation on your own, but if you turn everything over to The Lord He will work it out for you.

Today, take a stand and say that you are sick and tired of being sick and tired, and as of right now you will no longer let the enemy get the best of you. God says that you are a conqueror. (Romans 8:37) You will not be a victim but you will be a VICTOR! There is no need to be afraid anymore. He knows that you are suffering and He is quite aware that so many of you are living a life of pure hell. But please continue to be faithful, even to the point of death. Then God Himself will give you the Victor's Crown of Life! (Revelation 2:10)

"But thanks be to God, who gives us the victory through our Lord Jesus Christ." (1 Corinthians 15:57)

Blessed is the man who remains steadfast under trial, for when he has stood the test he will receive the crown of life, which God has promised to those who love him. (James 1:12)

At the end of the day:

_____
_____
_____
_____
_____
_____
_____

DECEMBER 9

GOD WILL SUSTAIN YOU

Life is hard. Somedays you just feel like it is more than you can bear. But even when you have reached old age with silver hair ,know that God made you and will carry you on. He will forever sustain and rescue you for all the days of your life. (Isaiah 46:4)

Today, no matter what you are dealing with, take comfort in knowing that God will be with you throughout your lifetime.

Remember, cast all of your cares on The Lord and He will sustain you. He will never let the righteous be shaken! (Psalm 55:22)

Behold, God is my helper; The Lord is the sustainer of my soul. (Psalm 54:4)

At the end of the day:

_____
_____
_____
_____
_____
_____
_____
_____
_____
_____
_____
_____

DECEMBER 10

GOD WILL SUPPLY

It's easy to get caught up and focus on the things that you need. Not even realizing that God has already supplied and taken care of all your needs. (Matthew 6:25)

Today stop worrying and stressing about your life. God has already supplied every need of yours according to His riches in glory in Christ Jesus. (Philippians 4:19)

Remember, it's already done! God, had you covered from the moment you had the problem.

But seek first the kingdom of God and his righteousness, and all these things will be added to you. (Matthew 6:33)

At the end of the day:

_____
_____
_____
_____
_____
_____
_____
_____
_____
_____
_____
_____

DECEMBER 11

GOD WILL STEP IN THE SITUATION

Often when you are pushed back into a corner, the situation that you are in can seem hopeless. It can make you feel as if you are alone and there is nothing you can do to get out of it. Good thing we know who sits on the throne! (Revelation 21:5)

Today know that while you are trying to figure it out God has already worked it out.

Remember, He works everything out for the good of those who love Him. (Romans 8:28)

Do you love Him?

Nor height nor depth, nor anything else in all creation, will be able to separate us from the love of God in Christ Jesus our Lord. (Romans 8:39)

At the end of the day:

_____
_____
_____
_____
_____
_____
_____
_____
_____
_____

DECEMBER 12

GOD PUTS PEOPLE IN YOUR LIFE FOR A REASON

Don't be so shocked and surprised by the fiery trial and storm that you are in. You might feel as if you can't take it no more and you don't understand why this is happening to you; but there is nothing going on in your life that is a surprise to God. (1 Peter 4:12) He has placed and designed everything to work together for your good. (Romans 8:28)

Sit back today and really think about your life. What feels like heartache, pain and suffering is just temporary. God has just set you up for your comeback through His people. This is all for your benefit so that the grace that is reaching more and more lives may cause thanksgiving to overflow to the glory of God. (2 Corinthians 4:15)

Don't get it twisted, God cannot be mocked. You will always harvest what you plant. (Galatians 6:7) God is going to bless those who are a blessing to you! (Genesis 12:3)

In him we were also chosen, having been predestined according to the plan of him who works out everything in conformity with the purpose of his will (Ephesians 1:11)

At the end of the day:

_____

_____

_____

_____

_____

_____

_____

DECEMBER 13

GOD IS TURNING IT AROUND

We know that all things work together for the good of those who love God, those who are called according to His purpose. (Romans 8:28) My dear friends, you have been faithful and your reward is coming. God has seen your suffering and heard your heartfelt cries for help. Every prayer that you prayed, He heard it and not one went unanswered. Don't think that for one moment God has forgotten about you or be surprised at the fiery trials you are going through, as if something strange were happening to you. (1 Peter 4:12) He is aware of everything that is taking place.

Today you don't have to fear because God is with you. Your situation has shifted in your favor. God has strengthened you, He is helping you, and He is holding you with His righteous right hand. (Isaiah 41:10)

Everything is going to be alright. There is nothing to fear.

God, has you!

Do you not know that you are God's temple and that God's Spirit dwells in you? (1 Corinthians 3:16)

At the end of the day:

_____
_____
_____
_____
_____
_____

DECEMBER 14

EVERY LITTLE STEP YOU TAKE

There is no need to worry what tomorrow may bring for your future. No need to keep trying to figure things out on your own. Today be at peace because before you even know it, God has already put into place whatever it is you need. If your situation didn't work out like you plan, again I say no need to worry, it just means He has something bigger and better in store.

God orders your steps, so always stay in Faith and put all your trust in Him and everything will be alright.

The steps of a good man are ordered by the Lord: and He delighted in His way. (Psalms 37:23)

At the end of the day:

_____
_____
_____
_____
_____
_____
_____
_____
_____
_____
_____
_____
_____

DECEMBER 15

Fight Fixed

Taking hits like you are a real heavyweight champion has been hard. Let's face it, the jabs and punches hurt; and you've been ducking and diving through it all. Little does the enemy know…that fight has already been fixed.

Today it's time to step out of the ring because the war is over. Quit arguing, tripping and acting a fool with someone when God has already called you victorious!

Remember, your faith will reveal that the fight was always fixed! (Tera Carissa)

Stand firm, and you will win life. (Luke 21:19)

At the end of the day:

_____
_____
_____
_____
_____
_____
_____
_____
_____
_____
_____
_____
_____
_____

DECEMBER 16

GET ON UP

Life gets very tough. It's "REAL". However, it's still no excuse for you not to, GET ON UP!

Right now put the Kleenex down and crawl out of bed if you need too. Your lying down in the bed isn't changing a thing! Put the phone DOWN! STOP complaining and telling the world about your situation and pray to God about your circumstances! You are stronger than you are giving yourself credit...STOP taking it personally and GET ON UP!

God is Not Attracted to Your Problems but he is attracted to Your Praise!

Today, You Need to...GET ON UP!

Arise, shine, for your light has come, and the glory of the Lord has risen upon you. (Isaiah 60:1)

At the end of the day:

_____
_____
_____
_____
_____
_____
_____
_____

DECEMBER 17

EXPECT IT!

The mindset that you wake up with is going to set the tone and stage for your day and future ahead. If you are thinking that God isn't going to turn it around, or you have already lost; you have just spoken defeat in the atmosphere.

Today and moving forward, have the mindset that I EXPECT God to work this out in my favor. I EXPECT this to turn around. I EXPECT God will have the last say. I EXPECT breakthroughs. I EXPECT this problem to cease and desist. I EXPECT God to be the lawyer, judge and jury. I EXPECT raises, bonuses, unexpected checks in the mail, sales, commissions, bills cancelled or decreased. EXPECT IT!!!!!!!! If you will decree it God will establish it for you, and light will shine on your ways. (Job 22:28)

Remember, if you have that mindset to EXPECT IT... Well, you ain't seen nothing yet!

Death and life are in the power of the tongue, and those who love it will eat its fruits." (Proverbs 18:21)

At the end of the day:

___
___
___
___
___
___
___

DECEMBER 18

EVEN WHEN IN DOUBT

There our times in our lives when we want to give up and throw in the towel; but God is still in the midst and says, Didn't I tell you that I wouldn't leave you nor forsake you? (Deuteronomy 31:6) So why are you doubting?

Today, you have to know that God loves you...and even when you didn't believe in yourself; He still believed in you!!!

Remember, doubt will kill more dreams than failure ever will!

You did not choose me, but I chose you and appointed you that you should go and bear fruit and that your fruit should abide, so that whatever you ask the Father in my name, He may give it to you. (John 15:16)

At the end of the day:

_____
_____
_____
_____
_____
_____
_____
_____
_____
_____
_____
_____

DECEMBER 19

DON'T STOP BELIEVING

When life is throwing you unfair blows and you seem to be robbing Peter to pay Paul; you can get discouraged and want to give up. But the devil is a lie, because you have faith in God. (Mark 11:22)

Today don't let the enemy in your head. Focus on the Word of The Lord. You can't get weary in this season; because at the proper time, you will reap if you don't give up. (Galatians 6:9)

Remember, you have come too far to give up now. Blessed are those who have not seen, but they still believe. So, keep believing and standing on God's promises; (John 20:29) because You will come out of this victorious!

May the God of hope fill you with all joy and peace in believing, so that by the power of the Holy Spirit you may abound in hope. (Romans 15:13)

At the end of the day:

___
___
___
___
___
___
___
___
___
___

DECEMBER 20

DON'T GET STUCK IN THE MOMENT

When you are in the midst of a storm, sometimes you get caught up in what is going on. You only see the situation through carnal eyes when you already know that it is a spiritual thing. Don't get stuck in your sad moment, your sad story and this sad time. Trouble doesn't last always and it won't rain forever.

Today let me tell you that God is the Author and the Finisher of your life. If you are at a low point right now, give God a mighty praise because your story is not going to end here in agony. God has a plan for your life. Plans to prosper you and not to harm you, plans to give you hope and a future. (Jeremiah 29:11)

Remember, Joseph wrongfully sat in prison before God moved him to the palace. So don't get stuck in the moment....Your palace and time are coming!

The LORD repays you for what you have done, and a full reward will be given to you by the LORD, the God of Israel, under whose wings you have come to take refuge! (Ruth 2:12)

At the end of the day:

_____
_____
_____
_____
_____
_____
_____

DECEMBER 21

BETTER DAYS ARE COMING

When you are going through, it is hard to see God in it with you. All you are focused and thinking about is what it looks and feels like. But The Lord himself goes before you and will be with you. He will never leave nor forsake you. There is no need to be afraid or discouraged anymore. God is walking this thing out with you. (Deuteronomy 31:8)

Today, rejoice in knowing that The Lord your God will bless you as he promised. He is on your side and there is nothing that a man or woman can do to you. (Psalm 118:6) You will no longer be the tail, but the head. As of right now you will lend and borrow from none. You will rule over many but they will not rule over you! (Deuteronomy 15:6)

Better Days are coming to YOU!

The LORD will open to you his good treasury, the heavens, to give the rain to your land in its season and to bless all the work of your hands. And you shall lend to many nations, but you shall not borrow. (Deuteronomy 28:12)

At the end of the day:

___
___
___
___
___
___

DECEMBER 22

BE STRONG WHILE YOU WAIT

In this life, you must be strong while you patiently wait for God to move in your life. You must know that The Lord is good to those who wait for Him and who seek Him. (Lamentations 3:25)

Today talk to God and ask Him for strength while you wait. I know if you look in the natural it might seem as if you can't do this, but the devil is a lie. You can do all things through Christ who gives you strength. (Philippians 4:13)

Remember, wait for the Lord and continue to be strong while you wait; and let your heart take courage!

But they who wait for the Lord shall renew their strength; they shall mount up with wings like eagles; they shall run and not be weary; they shall walk and not faint. (Isaiah 40:31)

At the end of the day:

_____
_____
_____
_____
_____
_____
_____
_____
_____

DECEMBER 23

A PEACE OF MIND IS PRICELESS

It is a horrible feeling when you feel as if you don't have a peace of mind. Day by day it can eat at you. God will keep those in perfect peace who trust Him and whose thoughts are on Him always. (Isaiah 26:3)

Today know that God has made it very clear that in Him we may have peace; but here in this world we are going to experience and have all kinds of trouble. However, we can take comfort in knowing that He has overcome the world. (John 16:33) It is the peace of God, which surpasses all understanding that will guard your hearts and your minds in Christ Jesus that will see you through. (Philippians 4:7)

Remember, God is not a God of confusion, but of peace. (1 Corinthians 14:33)

Now may the Lord of peace himself give you peace at all times, in every way. The Lord be with you all. (2 Thessalonians 3:16)

At the end of the day:

_____
_____
_____
_____
_____
_____
_____
_____
_____
_____

DECEMBER 24

A CHRISTMAS MIRACLE

The holidays are here, and in a couple of days we will be celebrating Christmas. The day our Savior was born. A time of joy and peace, but sadly to say, not everyone is in the Christmas spirit. A lot of people are depressed due to life's circumstances. It's hard for them to attend Christmas parties, sing Christmas songs and just get in the Holiday spirit. What they need is a Christmas Miracle.

I know you're in pain and I know you are hurting. But God didn't bring you this far to just leave you now. No matter what you are going through God is with you every step of the way. Just when you want to give up and throw in the towel, that's when your "suddenly" will take place.

Today, as you get the strength to try to make it through the holidays: Go into prayer and tell God what you are in need of and the miracle that your heart desires. Be reminded on why we celebrate Christmas. Start to praise and worship our Savior instead focusing on your situation. Before you know it, your Miracle will be in front of you.

Remember, that NOTHING is impossible for God! (Luke 1:37)

Jesus looked at them and said, "With man this is impossible, but with God all things are possible." (Matthew 19:26)

At the end of the day:

_____

_____

_____

_____

_____

DECEMBER 25

BEYOND THE LIGHTS

As many awake this morning and rush to the Christmas tree to see all the bright lights and shiny big boxes, keep in mind what we are truly representing.

So as you begin to open your gifts, sing your favorite Christmas carols and begin to eat your traditional holiday meals. Please don't forget that God has given all of us the best gift ever……His son Jesus Christ. (Luke 2:1-20)

Remember, beyond all the Christmas lights, carols, gifts and holiday meals. God's message for you and me is the same. YOU will have abundant life through Jesus Christ!

"Every good gift and every perfect gift is from above, coming down from the Father of lights with whom there is no variation or shadow due to change." (James 1:17)

Wishing All of You a Very Happy & Blessed Christmas.

To God Be The Glory ~

At the end of the day:

_____
_____
_____
_____
_____
_____
_____
_____

DECEMBER 26

AMAZING GRACE

For by grace you have been saved through faith, and this is not your own doing; it is the gift of God. (Ephesians 2:8) It is by the grace of God that you are who you are and where you are and it is not in vain. (1 Corinthians 15:10)

Today, know that it is grace that has saved, kept and protected you.

Remember, you are wrapped in God's grace!

And from his fullness we have all received, grace upon grace. (John 1:16)

At the end of the day:

DECEMBER 27

A HUNDREDFOLD RETURN

So many of us are going through in life and don't know what to do, so we just give up. But The Bible tells us that God doesn't want us to worry. We need to go to Him during life's raging storms.

Genesis 26:1 says that a famine was on its way to the land. And, of course, everyone went into panic mode...except Isaac. He trusted God and sowed seeds in the Land. And God blessed Him a hundredfold.

Today, I want you to know that I know it's hard when folks are mistreating you, talking about you, lying on you, walking out on you and giving up on you. But God says, "Be nice to them anyways. Don't sow the seeds they are throwing down." God is a very prosperous God and He will give you back and make up for all the wrongs and the famine you are enduring.

Remember, obey Him...and watch the walk of the wicked and the joy of His faithful servants!

"Bring the whole tithe into the storehouse, that there may be food in my house. Test me in this," says the LORD Almighty, "and see if I will not throw open the floodgates of heaven and pour out so much blessing that there will not be room enough to store it." (Malachi 3:10)

At the end of the day:

_____

_____

_____

_____

_____

DECEMBER 28

A MASTERPIECE

Just because you've gained a little weight or your situation has changed, there is no need to keep putting yourself down. You have to stop focusing on your flaws and know that the Creator says, "YOU are a masterpiece." (Ephesians 2:10)

Today it is time that you get in agreement with God and know that you are indeed what He says you are. The head and not the tail; and His very own prize possession!

Remember, you are not average and you are not ordinary...but YOU are God's Masterpiece!

I will give thanks to you, for I am fearfully and wonderfully made; Wonderful are Your works, And my soul knows it very well. (Psalm 139:14)

At the end of the day:

_____
_____
_____
_____
_____
_____
_____
_____
_____
_____

DECEMBER 29

A BLESSING IN EVERY LESSON

It can be hard when you are facing trying times. Oftentimes you will start to question why is God even allowing the storm in the first place.

Today, you need to know that in every trial, storm and heartbreak that you are enduring, God has reason for it. You may not understand it right now...but keep holding and see how God will work this thing out for your good.

Remember, the bad days that you are experiencing now will give you the best lessons of your life!

Trust in the Lord with all your heart, and do not lean on your own understanding. (Proverbs 3:5)

"Sometimes the cloud would stay over the Tabernacle for only a few days, so the people would stay for only a few days, as the Lord commanded. Then at the Lord's command they would break camp and move on." (Numbers 9:20)

At the end of the day:

_____
_____
_____
_____
_____
_____
_____
_____

DECEMBER 30

A MISTAKE OR A DECISION

When you start to do the same thing over and over; at some point, you have to realize it's no longer a mistake... but your decision to make.

Today you need to know that even though you may have lost and left some things; God can still reward and give you double for your trouble. Yes, the marriage, job and relationship didn't work out. But keep looking ahead to what God is about to spring forth in your life. (Isaiah 43:19)

Remember, a mistake repeated more than once is a decision. (Paul Coelho)

"If any of you lacks wisdom, let him ask God, who gives generously to all without reproach, and it will be given him." (James 1:5)

At the end of the day:

_____
_____
_____
_____
_____
_____
_____
_____
_____
_____

DECEMBER 31

A BATTLE TURNED INTO A BLESSING

Although the waves of the storm you are in are raging high, know that God does everything for a reason, and He doesn't put more on you than you can bear. If you are in it, it is because God has a blessing with your name on it and you must endure it for a minute.

Today, have confidence in knowing that yes, you may walk through the darkest valley, but His rod and staff are there with you. (Psalm 23:4)

Remember, from dark clouds we get precious water. From dark mines, we get valuable jewels, and from our darkest trials come our biggest and best blessings from God.

"And after you have suffered a little while, the God of all grace, who has called you to his eternal glory in Christ, will himself restore, confirm, strengthen, and establish you." (1 Peter 5:10)

At the end of the day:

ABOUT THE AUTHOR

Travasa Buford is a Henderson KY native and resides now in Huntsville AL. She has been in advertising for 20 years and is currently the Digital Media Manager for WZDX News. In 2010 she launched, hosted and co-produced, "My Color is Beautiful". A half hour show dedicated to women and men of color on WEHT NEWS 25 an ABC affiliate in Henderson KY.

Travasa is a member of Eagles' Nest Ministries Church under the leadership of Bishop Daniel J. Richardson, where she oversees the Media Ministry. She also handles the Media Ministry for her home church that she is close with in Evansville IN, New Hope Missionary Baptist church under the leadership of Pastor Rabon L. Turner Sr. She is very active in the community by mentoring young girls and speaking with women that are going through various trials and storms.

Travasa also writes daily Devotionals that reach thousands of people every day from her ministry, TNHB Inspirations.

For speaking engagements and purchases you may contact the author

Web:
www.tnhb-inspirations.com

Facebook:
www.facebook.com/tnhb-inspirations
@TNHBInspirations

Instagram:
www.instagram.com/tnhb_inspirations
tnhb_inspirations

Email:
tnhb.inspirations@yahoo.com

www.ingramcontent.com/pod-product-compliance
Lightning Source LLC
Chambersburg PA
CBHW071852290426
44110CB00013B/1113